W9-AEP-152

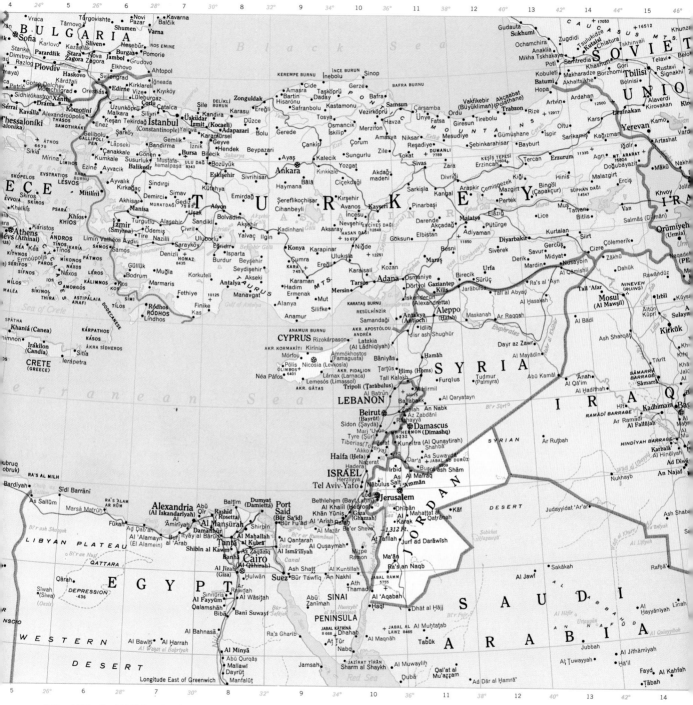

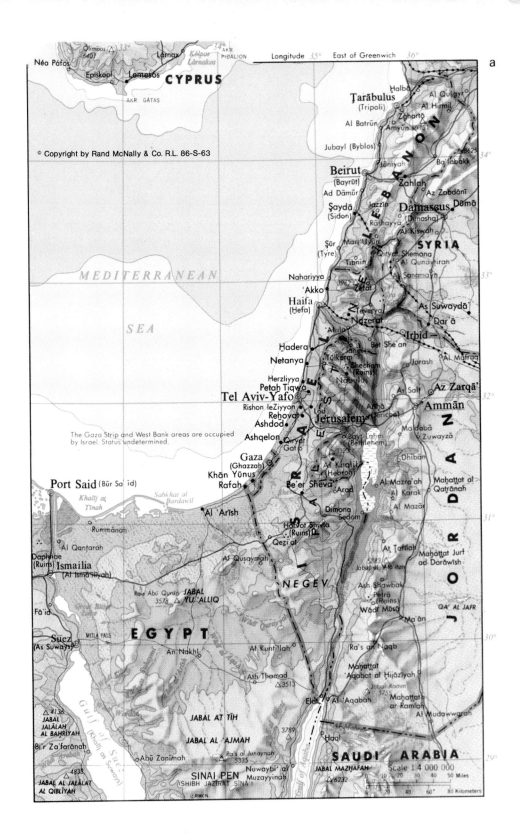

CYPRUS

Néa Páfos
Olimbos △133°
6401
Larnax
Kólpor
Lárnakos
AKR.
PIBALION
Episkopí
Lemesós
AKR. GÁTAS

Longitude 35° East of Greenwich 36°

a

Ţarābulus
(Tripoli)
Halbā
Al Qusayr
Al Hirmil
Al Batrūn
Zghortā
Amyūn
Jubayl (Byblos)
△2825
Bā'labakk
34°

MEDITERRANEAN

Beirut
(Bayrūt)
Jūniyah
LEBANON
Ad Dāmūr
Zahlah
Az Zabdānī
Şaydā
(Sidon)
Jazzīn
Damascus
Dūmā
(Dimashq)
Rāshayyā
Al Kiswah
Şūr
(Tyre)
Marj 'Uyūn
SYRIA
Tibnīn
Qiryat Shemona
Al Qunayţirah
△3942
Nahariyya
Zefat
As Sanamayn
33°

'Akko
Ţeverya
As Suwaydā'
SEA
Haifa
(Hefa)
Nazerat
Dar'ā
'Atula
Bet She'an
Irbid
Hadera
Jenin
Al Mafraq
Netanya
Ţūlkarm
Shechem
(Ruins)
Jarash
Herzliyya
Nabulus
Petah Tiqwa
As Salt
Az Zarqā'
Tel Aviv-Yafo
Lod
Amman
Rishon leZiyyon
Jericho
Rehovot
Jerusalem
32°
Ashdod
Madaba
Bayt Lahm
Az Zuwayzā
Ashqelon
(Bethlehem)
Qiryat
Gat
Dhibān
Gaza
Al Khalil
(Ghazzah)
(Hebron)
Khān Yūnus
Be'er Sheva
Al Mazra'ah
Mahattat al
Rafah
Arad
Al Karak
Qatrānah
Dimona
Al Mazār
Sedom
31°
Port Said (Būr Sa'id)
Al 'Arīsh
Horvot Shivta
Khalīj aţ
(Ruins)
Tīnah
Sabkhat al
Bardawīl
Qezi'ot
At Tafīlah
Rummānah
Mahattat Jurt
ad Darāwīsh
Al Qanţarah
Al Qusaymah
5383
Daphnae
Jabal al 'Arā'ton
(Ruins) Ismailia
Ash Shawbak
(Al Ismā'īliyah)
NEGEV
Petra
Fā'id
(Ruins)
Wādī Mūsā
Ra's Abū Qurūn
JABAL
Ma'ān
3578 △ YU 'ALLIQ
QA' AL JAFR
Süez
(As Suways)
E G Y P T
Ra's an Naqb
An Nakhl
JORDAN
Al Kuntillah
Mahattat
'Aqabat al Hijāzīyah
△4136
575
Ath Thamad
△3513
Jabal Ramm
Mahattat
JABAL
ar Ramlah
JALĀLAH
Elat
Al 'Aqabah
Al Mudawwarah
AL BAHRĪYAH
3789
Bi'r Za'farānah
△
Haql
JABAL AT TĪH
JABAL AL 'AJMAH
△4838
Abū Zanīmah
Ra's al Junaynah
SAUDI ARABIA
JABAL JALĀLAT
5335
Scale 1:4 000 000
AL QIBLĪYAH
SINAI PEN
Nuwaybi' al
JABAL MAZHAFAH
29°
(SHIBH JAZĪRAT SĪNĀ')
Muzayyinah
△6232

The Gaza Strip and West Bank areas are occupied
by Israel. Status undetermined.

Scale 1:4 000 000
0 10 20 30 40 50 Miles
0   40   60'   80 Kilometers

Enchantment of the World

ISRAEL

By Helen Hinckley Jones

Consultant for Israel: Bernard Reich, Ph.D., Professor, Department of Political Science, George Washington University, Washington, D.C.

Consultant for Reading: Robert L. Hillerich, Ph.D., Bowling Green State University, Bowling Green, Ohio

CHILDRENS PRESS ®

CHICAGO

A rabbi prays at the Western Wall.

Picture Acknowledgments
H. Armstrong Roberts: Cover, pages 43, 53 (top), 55 (left), 115 (left); © M. Koene: Pages 53 (bottom), 59, 88;
© Blumenbild: Page 5; © Westebbe/ZEFA: Page 24;
© ZEFA/U.K.: Page 28; © Benser/ZEFA: Page 44 (bottom);
© R. Krubner: Page 47; © Starfoto/ZEFA: Pages 50, 111;
© Camerique: Page 91 (top right)
Photri: Pages 4, 65, 67 (right), 70, 71, 78 (right), 80 (bottom left), 83 (right), 86, 110
Nawrocki Stock Photo: © James A. Cudney: Pages 6, 8, 17 (bottom right), 18, 23, 27 (top right), 34, 67 (left), 75 (right), 117; © Anthony Russo: Pages 60 (left), 62
Historical Pictures Service, Inc., Chicago: Pages 9, 11, 12, 98
© **Joan Dunlop:** Pages 15, 37 (left)
© **Chandler Forman:** Pages 17 (bottom left), 20, 37 (right), 75 (left), 96, 107
Root Resources: © W. Helfrich: Pages 17 (top), 105 (left); © Evelyn R. Davidson: Pages 21, 30 (left); © Mary Gray: Page 108
Third Coast Stock Source/Variations in Photography: © Zave Smith: Pages 27 (top left and bottom), 79; © Eugene G. Schulz: Page 54
The Photo Source International: Pages 30 (right), 35, 80 (top), 91 (top left), 92 (left), 105 (right), 116
© **Cameramann International, Ltd.:** Pages 33, 44 (top), 61, 64, 72, 76, 78 (left), 80 (bottom right), 83 (left), 91 (bottom left and right), 92 (right), 94
Wide World Photos: Pages 36, 40, 41, 100, 101, 104
Marilyn Gartman Agency: © Michael Philip Manheim: Pages 55 (right), 60 (right), 93 (right), 115 (right)
© **Emilie Lepthien:** Page 56
© **Erwin Pickard:** Pages 57, 93 (left), 106
Len Meents: Maps on pages 53, 64, 66, 70
Courtesy Flag Research Center, Winchester, Massachusetts 01890: Flag on back cover
Cover: The Church of All Nations in Jerusalem

Library of Congress Cataloging-in-Publication Data

Jones, Helen Hinckley, 1903-
    Israel.

    (Enchantment of the world)
    Includes index.
    Summary: A history of Israel and a description of its cities, its people, its customs, and its indomitable spirit.
    1. Israel—Juvenile literature. [1. Israel]
I. Title. II. Series.
DS102.95.J66   1986   956.94   85-5740
ISBN 0-516-02766-2

A Bedouin couple in the Negev Desert

TABLE OF CONTENTS

Chapter 1

IN THE BEGINNING

Jerusalem, the Holy City, is sacred to Jews, Christians, and Muslims. There is a Jewish legend that says Jerusalem is the cornerstone of the whole earth: "The Almighty, blessed be He, dropped a rock in the waters and from there the whole world expanded." In some ancient maps of the world the Holy Land is the center, and other nations, even continents, are grouped around it.

WHEN HISTORY WAS WRITTEN IN RUINS

While the people of Israel date from about 3,500 years ago, the land of Israel is much older. Digging down to the deepest levels, archaeologists have found amazing things. Perhaps 250,000 years ago the land was covered with ice. During that time people lived in caves to protect themselves from the cold. The blackened openings of caves are still seen on Mount Carmel and in the Galilean hills.

When the ice melted, great forests grew. It is hard to imagine that enormous animals such as elephants and rhinoceroses lived there, but archaeologists have found their bones. By 7500 B.C.

Opposite: A portion of a model of Jerusalem as the ancient city looked at the time of Christ

Excavations at the Jericho tell have revealed evidence of ancient cultures.

some of the people had settled in towns, giving up their lives as nomadic herdsmen for agriculture and simple trades. Jericho, not far north of the Dead Sea, is estimated to be ten thousand years old. It may be the oldest city in the world. We know about this early city from the tell.

A tell is a man-made mountain. In a place where there has been water and fertile soil, a new town would be built on top of a ruined one. When this town was destroyed another was built on top of it. This went on for thousands of years until a great mound was built. Each town's ruins tell us about a different advance in civilization. By cutting down through a tell we can find out about the culture of each period by the utensils, tools, and other artifacts that the people living then left behind. In the lowest level of the Jericho tell are the remains of a charcoal fire. By measuring the amount of radioactivity that is left in this material, scientists can tell, within three hundred years or so, the date of the ruins.

Israel dates from the time that Abraham, with his flocks and herds, settled in the land of Canaan.

FATHER ABRAHAM

But this early Jericho wasn't Israel. Israel began when Abraham with his flocks and herds came from Ur on the Fertile Crescent to the land that God had promised to him and his people. According to the Bible, Abraham went into the land of Canaan and settled there because it was the Promised Land.

This is important to the story of Israel. God made a covenant, or agreement, with Abraham to give the land of Canaan to him and his descendants in return for their obedience. This covenant was different from other agreements. It was between God and Abraham. It was this covenant that the people of Israel pointed to (and some still point to it) to justify their right to settle permanently on the land.

MOSES THE LAWGIVER

Abraham had two sons—Ishmael and Isaac. Isaac's son Jacob was called Israel. Jacob named a tribe for each of his twelve sons. From his son Judah's name, the people came to be called Jews and the area in which they lived, Judea. The country later came to be called Israel, Jacob's special name.

Jacob's young son Joseph was so favored by his father that his older brothers were jealous and sold him into slavery in Egypt. There his wisdom saved Egypt from famine and he won recognition from the pharaoh. When the famine reached Canaan, Jacob and his other sons went into Egypt and settled in Goshen. In Egypt the descendants of Abraham were happy until a new pharaoh came to power and made them slaves.

In 1280 B.C. Moses, an Israelite by birth, was called to lead the Israelites out of Egypt and slavery. After forty years of wandering, Moses and his people finally reached the Promised Land.

One of the most dramatic moments in this journey was the hour when, according to the Scriptures, Moses received the Ten Commandments on Mount Sinai. No doubt the people were already acquainted with many of these commandments, but a codification of the law was something different. The people made a covenant with God to live by these commandments.

Though the account of the Israelites' journey is found only in the Bible, parts of it have been substantiated by archaeology. For instance, an excavated tell near Arad in the Negev Desert disclosed the remains of the fort from which soldiers must have attacked Moses, as the Book of Numbers relates. It was the strong defense of Arad that made Moses take a long route by way of Jericho and enter Canaan from the east.

Moses with the Ten Commandments

A COVENANT PEOPLE

Although Moses led the people on their long travels out of Egypt, it was Joshua who took them into the Promised Land (1250-1200 B.C.). Joshua conquered a large part of Canaan. In Shechem the covenant between God and His people was written on stone and placed in an ark (box), and the ark was placed in a tabernacle (tent). It is this covenant, deep in the hearts of the people, that has carried them through many difficult centuries.

At first the people retained their tribal government. Each tribe's business and political affairs were handled by the oldest man in the tribe, the patriarch. After a time these tribal groups gave way to a loose federation of judges. As Israel became an urban, agricultural society and as tribes of Philistines began to push in on them, the people demanded a king. The priest-prophet Samuel named Saul to be king. Saul, who reigned from from about 1020 to 1005 B.C., was a great warrior. He battled successfully against the Philistines, who controlled a portion of the Mediterranean coast and looked enviously at the rich land the Israelites controlled.

11

King David made Jerusalem his capital and brought to the city the Ark of the Covenant, which contained the tablets on which were written the Ten Commandments.

DAVID, SINGER AND WARRIOR

David, the next king, expanded the kingdom of Israel (1004-928 B.C.). He was the first Israelite to conquer Jerusalem and he made the city his capital. From Jerusalem he led his conquering armies far and wide until his kingdom reached from the Euphrates River on the east to Egypt on the west.

When David's son King Solomon took over this extended kingdom (965-922 B.C.), he built the first temple in Jerusalem and established elaborate rituals in it. He also built royal palaces and good roads. Solomon was renowned for his great wisdom in governing his people and in settling disputes fairly.

Literature—the Psalms ascribed to David, the Proverbs to Solomon—was written, as were history, stories, and dramas. Jerusalem became one of the trade centers of the world. But taxes were high, the army had become a mercenary force, the government was bureaucratic, and the people were little better than slaves.

THE DIVIDED KINGDOM

Solomon's kingdom lasted only briefly after his death. Israel split into the Northern Kingdom, consisting of ten tribes, and the Southern Kingdom, with the tribes of Benjamin and Judah. The Northern Kingdom lasted only until 721 B.C., and had twenty kings in less than two hundred years. Sargon II of Assyria conquered and destroyed Israel, carrying off the ten tribes of the Northern Kingdom to exile and obscurity.

The Southern Kingdom, Judah, lasted a little longer. Old Testament prophets thundered warnings that Judah would surely be destroyed if the people did not live up to their covenant. The prophets had predicted the fall of Israel to Assyria; now they warned of Judah's fall to Babylon. But in spite of these warnings, the Babylonians destroyed Judah (597 B.C.). Solomon's temple was demolished and the people were taken captive into Babylon.

CYRUS OF PERSIA, THE FIRST HUMANITARIAN

Then a wonderful thing happened. Cyrus the Great of Persia conquered Babylonia. He freed the Jews held captive there and told them to return to Jerusalem (538 B.C.). Most of the Jews gladly responded. By 520 B.C. those who had returned had begun to rebuild Solomon's temple. In five years it was dedicated. In 445 B.C. the new city walls of Jerusalem were completed. This didn't mean that Judah was independent. Persia still controlled it but left the government in the hands of governors, who proved to be unstable. When in 445 B.C. Nehemiah and Ezra established a government based on the Pentateuch (the first five books of the Bible), stability was finally achieved. The society was controlled by the temple priesthood, and the ruler was a single high priest who was a direct descendant of Aaron. (Aaron was the brother of Moses and spoke as his "mouthpiece.")

During the time that the high priests governed Jerusalem, Alexander the Great of Macedonia conquered Persia, and with Persia Judah fell into his hands. When Alexander died, his enormous kingdom was divided among his great generals. Both Ptolemy of Egypt and the Seleucids of Syria wanted to control the eastern Mediterranean region of Palestine.

THE HASMONEAN PERIOD

When Alexander the Great, the Ptolemies, and some of Seleucids ruled, the Jews attempted to get along with their rulers. After all, they were accustomed to having a foreign power control them. But when the Seleucid Antiochus IV Epiphanes came into power things became unendurable. He demanded that the Jews adopt Greek customs and even worship the Greek god Zeus in their holy temple. To ask this of a people who had long before replaced many gods with one God, who believed that their temple was the home of the "Sacred Presence," was preposterous.

The priest Mattathias, of the Maccabees family, announced, "Whoever is zealous of the law let him follow me." Jews who were eager to defeat Antiochus IV had found their leader. Mattathias had five sons, all of whom followed their father into battle. It was Judas Maccabaeus, the third son, who had the military genius to lead the Jews to victory and independence in the 160s B.C. The Maccabees, also known as the Hasmoneans, then governed Judea for the next century.

If only it could have lasted! But in the first century B.C. Rome

This Roman aqueduct stands in the city of Caesaria, which Herod built in 22 B.C.

was busy conquering the known world. The Roman legions, under Pompey, captured Jerusalem in 63 B.C. and executed the last Hasmonean king in 37 B.C.

The Romans dominated Palestine from 63 B.C. to A.D 324. They ruled through puppet kings, through appointed procurators, and through the Jewish council of judges and administrators known as the Sanhedrin.

Especially interesting is the reign of Herod, from 37 B.C. to 4 B.C. The son of the adviser to the last Hasmonean, he took the Roman side against his own people in order to gain personal power. Herod was a great builder. He built a splendid temple in Jerusalem, a powerful fortress at Herodion, and another fortress and palaces at Masada by the Dead Sea.

There were turbulent years in the first century A.D. Many young dissidents gathered followers around them. Among these was Jesus of Nazareth. His followers believed that he was the long-awaited Messiah and called him "King of the Jews." This title was seen as a threat to the government, and the Roman procurator, Pontius Pilate, allowed him to be put to death.

Instead of dying with Jesus' death, his teachings were carried to Asia Minor and the Mediterranean world by Saul of Tarsus, whose name was changed to Paul. His message was appealing to a growing number of people—particularly to non-Jews, or gentiles—but the teachings of Jesus were little felt in Jerusalem.

In A.D. 66 the provocative acts of the Roman procurators sent the Jews again into open defiance. Rome swore to destroy Jerusalem and the temple that the Jews had built after their return from captivity in Babylonia. The Jews fought courageously but the temple was destroyed in the year 70 and countless Jews were killed.

Yet the Jews, with the feeling that this was their Promised Land, wouldn't give up. They worshiped in the ruins of their temple and in 132, led by Bar Kokhba, they revolted against Roman Emperor Hadrian. Again they were unsuccessful. Hadrian recalled his troops from Great Britain and swore to destroy Jerusalem. He ordered that it be "ploughed up with a yoke of oxen." Even historical names were changed. The city built where Jerusalem had stood was named Aelia Capitolina. No Jews were allowed to enter.

This model of Herod's temple (above) is part
of the ancient Jerusalem exhibit at the Holyland
Hotel in West Jerusalem. A great builder, Herod
also built a powerful fortress at Herodion (below)
and another fortress and palaces at Masada by the
Dead Sea.

When Jesus of Nazareth was sentenced to death,
he was taken along a path (left) that is now
called the Via Dolorosa (Street of Sorrows) to his
place of execution at Golgotha.

The Church of the Holy Sepulcher, standing on what is believed to be the site of Christ's tomb, is one of the many churches built by Constantine the Great, a converted Christian.

THE FIRST CHRISTIAN RULER

When Constantine the Great became emperor in 324, barbarians from the north were endangering Rome. Constantine moved his capital to Byzantia at the eastern end of the Mediterranean, making it the center of world power and culture. A converted Christian, Constantine also made Christianity the official religion of the Roman Empire. This influence, of course, reached Palestine.

When Constantine's mother, Helena, visited Jerusalem, all that was left of the original city was part of the temple wall called the Western Wall. To honor her, Constantine built churches and monasteries on sacred Christian sites. He built the Church of the Holy Sepulcher, on the site where earlier conquerors had built a temple to Venus, and the Church of the Nativity in Bethlehem. For the next three centuries, Christians were encouraged to settle in Jerusalem, but Jews were allowed to enter only once a year. In 614 the Persians, with a new burst of power, invaded Palestine and, aided by Jews, were successful in seizing it from the Romans. The Persians, like the earlier Cyrus the Great, gave the Jews freedom to enter their holy city and to rule themselves.

THE ARABS AND ISLAM

In the seventh century a new movement arose from the east. An Arab named Muhammad, born in Mecca and living for a time in Medina, was preaching a new religion called Islam. According to Islam, there was one god, Allah, and Muhammad was his prophet, or spokesman. Islam had many features in common with Judaism and Christianity, such as monotheism, or belief in one god. It also taught ethical standards, forbidding lying, stealing, adultery, and murder. Islam's holy book, the Koran, contains not only the teachings of Muhammad but also religious stories about Jesus and many Old Testament prophets, who are also honored as prophets by Muslims, or followers of Islam.

One of the tenets of the new religion, however, was the *jihad*, a holy war to spread the belief in Allah and his prophet. And so, fired by their faith, Arab warriors set out to spread Islam throughout the world, beginning in the Middle East, North Africa, and southern Europe.

Jerusalem fell to the Muslims in 638. It was already the Holy City of Jews and Christians. But during the Islamic occupation

The Dome of the Rock is located on a site that is holy to both Jews and Muslims.

Jerusalem grew to become a holy city of Islam as well, as many Judeo-Christian holy places were converted to Islamic shrines. The Dome of the Rock, for instance, was built over the Moriah Rock. This stone was believed to be the altar on which Abraham was to have sacrificed his son Isaac to God and also the location of the sacred chamber of the destroyed temple called the Holy of Holies. But for Muslims it was also the stone from which Muhammad ascended into heaven. Near the Dome of the Rock, too, had been a Christian basilica dedicated to the Virgin. It was converted to El Aqsa Mosque. Both structures remain holy places for devout Muslims even today.

Though Jews and Christians became second-class citizens under the Islamic occupation, they were generally tolerated by the various Arab groups that controlled Palestine over the next four centuries. However, when the Turkish Seljuks came into power in the eleventh century, Christian pilgrims on their way to Jerusalem were attacked, beaten, and robbed. Sacred buildings were destroyed or desecrated. The emperor at Constantinople appealed to Pope Urban II for help, and thus began the Crusades.

This ancient Crusader fortress on an island in the Red Sea near Eilat was built entirely of coral rock.

THE CRUSADES

In 1099, the Crusaders took Jerusalem. When they entered the city they fell upon their knees and kissed the ground. Then in a most un-Christian manner they massacred not only Muslims, but Jews and even Christians. New laws and customs were introduced—the laws and customs of France. After the first Crusade was a success, the Crusaders stayed in Jerusalem with the hope of making it completely Christian and European.

In 1187 Saladin, the sultan of Egypt, joined the Muslims' war against the Christians. His columns defeated the Christians and he held Jerusalem, but he made a treaty with the Christians that would allow them to visit the Holy Land without injury. Saladin invited the Christians and Jews to worship as they pleased. He made an effort to stabilize the country, but his success brought about the Third Crusade. When Richard the Lion-Hearted attempted another Crusade he took only one city, Acre. The European Christians tried again and again—there were seven Crusades in all—but none but the first was successful.

In 1291 the last of the Crusaders were driven out of Acre. The Crusades were over and the Muslims held the Holy Land, including Jerusalem.

Jerusalem rested, decayed. There were no powerful leaders, no stable government, no one who seemed to care that walls were tumbling, buildings were collapsing, no progress was being made.

In 1520 Suleiman the Magnificent came to power in the Turkish Ottoman Empire. Though his capital was Constantinople, he really cared about Jerusalem. He rebuilt the crumbling walls, though not exactly where they had been built before. He conducted a stable government and was fair to the Jews, whom he welcomed to their Promised Land. Encouraged by peace and stability, people began to rebuild their homes. Villages and towns began to prosper.

Toward the end of the seventeenth century, after almost two hundred years of prosperity, the Ottoman Empire had trouble at home and was forced to withdraw its support from Palestine. Bandits, particularly in Galilee, began to harass the people. Jerusalem was not well governed and the taxes were so high that people fled the city.

Being exiled was nothing new to the Jews, nor was fleeing from persecution. The Diaspora—the scattering of the Jews outside the land of Israel—actually began when Solomon's temple was destroyed in 587 B.C. The victorious Babylonians took exiles to Babylonia, and when Cyrus the Great of Persia conquered Babylonia and allowed these exiles to return to Jerusalem, many of them chose to stay. Refugee Jews also found homes in Asia Minor, Egypt, Greece, and Rome. When the apostle Paul took the journeys recounted in the New Testament, he found Jews everywhere he went.

Mount Zion (above), in southeastern Jerusalem, has been revered traditionally as the site of King David's tomb and of the Last Supper.

The misplaced Jews began to participate in all of the occupations of the expanding society, including world trade and world finance. In Andalusia in southern Spain, Jews found a place in every occupation from agriculture to trade, and from high political position to the writing of poetry.

There were only brief periods in history when Palestine could shape Jewish thought and activity. Still, through all of the bitter, changing times, Jerusalem stood as the spiritual center of Israel; still, Mount Zion was the symbol of the Promised Land.

The Crusaders' castle at Belvoir commands this spectacular view of the Jordan Valley.

Chapter 2

THE LAND OF PROMISE

Israel is a very small country, rich in history and in promise. Under King David and his son, King Solomon, it reached from the Euphrates River to Egypt. Now it is a fraction of its former size. Along the Jordan River is a strip of land called the West Bank, which Jordan controlled from 1949 to 1967 and which Israel has controlled since then. This strip is twice as wide as Israel and almost a third as long. But the West Bank aside, Israel is only about 10 miles (16 kilometers) wide at its narrowest point. A good jogger could cross Israel at this point in less than an hour.

From the northern boundary, where a small neck of land juts up between Lebanon and Syria, to the southernmost tip that touches the Gulf of Aqaba, Israel is just 256 miles (412 kilometers) long. There are a little over 8,000 square miles (20,720 square kilometers) in all of Israel, with the southern portion covered by the Negev Desert. In 1986, 4,200,000 people lived in this country.

Israel's neighbors are Lebanon, which continues north along the Mediterranean coast, Syria to the northeast, Jordan to the east, and Egypt to the southwest. Neighboring Arab states to the east and the north that have refused to recognize Israel and have tried to destroy it have been an important part of the recent history of the homeland of the Jews. Egypt, which signed a peace treaty with Israel in 1979, has had an important share in Israel's history as well.

MOUNTAINS AND DESERT

No matter what kind of country you like, you will find it in Israel. Galilee is a mountainous country with pleasant valleys, valleys rich enough to make any farmer happy. There are the hills of Judea and Samaria in the West Bank; and there are the Plains of Sharon along the Mediterranean coast, where citrus trees grow in the subtropical climate. There are over 100 miles (161 kilometers) of coastline with sand and sea, ports, and rich industrial complexes; and there is the Negev Desert.

The Negev Desert is shaped like an arrow with its southern tip on the Gulf of Aqaba. The other end of the arrow is an imaginary line drawn from Gaza east through Beersheba.

Israel borders four bodies of water: the Mediterranean Sea on the west, the Sea of Galilee (also known as Lake Tiberias) in the northern hills, the Dead Sea in the Negev, and the Gulf of Aqaba at the tip of the Negev. There are three important rivers. The Jordan rises near the borders of Israel, Lebanon, and Syria. Now, in its old age, it loops and flows 165 miles (266 kilometers) from the Sea of Galilee to the Dead Sea 60 miles (97 kilometers) away. The Qishon River flows into the Mediterranean near Haifa. The Yarqon, much farther south, flows into the Mediterranean near Tel Aviv. The Jordan and Yarqon furnish water for irrigation projects in the upper Negev. The irrigation system known as the National Water Carrier also pipes water from the Sea of Galilee to the desert.

The Sinai Mountains (above left), on the Sinai Peninsula southwest of Israel, are
the site of a number of Old Testament events. The Negev Desert (above right)
and the Mediterranean coast (below) are features of Israel's richly varied landscape.

The hot, dry climate of Eilat, on the arm of the Red Sea called the Gulf of Aqaba, attracts vacationers from Israel and Europe.

WINTER AND SUMMER

Any kind of weather can be found, even beautiful summer the year around, by traveling from the north to the south. There is usually a cool breeze in upper Galilee, and Jerusalem is generally pleasant. For a climate similar to the European Mediterranean resorts, spend time on the coast at Tel Aviv, Haifa, or Acre. For warm, dry winters and scuba diving among the most beautiful fish in the world, there is always the Gulf of Aqaba.

Even sandstorms are available. The parching hot desert wind called the *Sharav* can raise early summer temperatures as high as 122 degrees Fahrenheit (50 degrees Celsius).

In the summer, from April to October, there is little rain. The winter is the rainy season. During the winter months there may be cyclonic westerlies when the rain comes down in sheets instead of drops. If the water isn't controlled it carries away valuable soils. But this doesn't happen in every part of Israel. There is a variation in rainfall from the north to the south and from the east to the west. In the mountains of Galilee the average annual rainfall is almost 40 inches (102 centimeters). Haifa on the coast has 25 inches (64 centimeters); Jerusalem, inland, 20 inches (51 centimeters). Is there snow? Well, sometimes. Snow comes infrequently to Jerusalem, more frequently to the mountains of Galilee. But there is enough snow in the northeast for ski resorts to flourish.

The temperature depends, of course, on where you are. There are three factors. The first is how far north or south you are, the second on how near the coast, the third on the elevation. Upper Galilee is 3,963 feet (1,208 meters) above sea level. As you move south the elevation drops and is between 2,000 and 1,000 feet (610 and 305 meters). A good measure of change in elevation is the Jordan River. At the northernmost boundary of Israel, at Dan, the river is 500 feet (152 meters) above sea level. When it enters the Sea of Galilee it is already 690 feet (210 meters) below. When it enters the Dead Sea it is 1,302 feet (397 meters) below sea level. The Dead Sea is the lowest sea in the world, and it is eight times as salty as the ocean.

How is it that the Jordan River is so much lower than the land? There is a steep slope from the land to the river.

Sometime, in ages past, there was a deep rift made by movement of the earth through which the Jordan found its way.

But the weather? The temperature is seldom more than 100 degrees Fahrenheit (37.8 degrees Celsius) in Jerusalem. Much of the Jordan River valley is hot, and the Negev is extremely hot. But on the coast there is beautiful weather. In Tel Aviv it seldom gets

Near the ancient Roman city of Tiberias (right), a modern kibbutz produces crops that are sold in city markets (left).

hotter than 90 degrees Fahrenheit (32.2 degrees Celsuis) or lower than 50 degrees Fahrenheit (10 degrees Celsius).

So that is Israel. It has mountains and hills, plains and deserts, seas of sweet water and seas of salt. How can there be such variation in such a small land? In Israel there is everything from the richest accounts of ancient history laced with legend, to the most highly developed farming methods, the best in education and culture.

How can Israel, so small, have so much?

Chapter 3

ISRAEL TODAY

Today's Israel was born in the mind of Theodor Herzl and in the hearts of the Russian Jews who had organized the "Love of Zion" movement.

Herzl was born in Budapest, Hungary, and brought up without the traditional Jewish background. Although he studied law, he became a journalist. He was in Paris at the time that an innocent Jew, Alfred Dreyfus, was sentenced to Devil's Island after being falsely accused of betraying military information to the enemy. Anti-Semitism, or prejudice against Jews, wasn't something that would go away, Herzl felt. It was something so deeply ingrained that the only way that Jews could live up to their potential was to form a state of their own. In 1896 he published *The Jewish State*. The state that he dreamed of would be progressive and modern. It was not important where this state was located as long as it was independent. But he felt that the traditional location, in the Holy Land, would be most logical.

In 1881 there had been a massacre of Jews in Russia. Survivors began to think of themselves as Jews rather than Russians. There was also deep suffering among Jews in Romania. The "Love of Zion" movement became stronger as more Jews felt the racial bias, the anti-Semitic fever in Europe.

When Herzl heard of the "Love of Zion" movement, he felt certain that the dreamed-of Jewish state should be in Palestine. He believed Palestine was "a country without a people." He urged the nations of the world to give it to "a people without a country."

Herzl organized the First Zionist Congress in Basel, Switzerland, in 1897. This marked the beginning of political Zionism, the movement toward the creation of an independent Jewish homeland. Herzl was a natural leader, but many Jews opposed political Zionism. Some felt that Jews should remain a religious group rather than a political group. Others believed that only the coming of the Messiah could restore the Jews to Zion.

Meanwhile, Jewish immigration (called *aliyah*, "ascent to the land") into Palestine continued, until by 1914 there were 85,000 Jews in the area.

World War I provided an opportunity for the Zionist movement to promote its goals. Chaim Weizmann, a noted British chemist and a leader of the Zionist movement, helped persuade Britain to adopt the Balfour Declaration in November 1917. It read, in part: "His Majesty's Government view with favour the establishment in Palestine of a national home for the Jewish people, and will use their best endeavours to facilitate the achievement of this object, it being clearly understood that nothing shall be done which may prejudice the civil and religious rights of existing non-Jewish communities in Palestine, or the rights and political status enjoyed by Jews in any other country."

Britain succeeded in liberating the Middle East from the Turks in 1917, and on December 11, British General Allenby entered Jerusalem. The Jews rushed to join the Allied forces. Perhaps now the way would be open to form the state that Herzl and thousands

Lush agricultural settlements, now found even in the Negev Desert, show the determination of the Jewish immigrants to transform the poor land they had found in their new country.

of others had dreamed of. In the Balfour Declaration, the British had expressed support for a Jewish national home in Palestine. So the League of Nations gave the mandate to oversee Palestine to the British, who were to work toward fulfillment of the Balfour Declaration pledge.

What sort of land were the immigrants coming to? It was a poverty-stricken spot. When the ancient forests were cut down, the soil had been allowed to erode from the slopes. Sand dunes piled along the coast kept the streams from emptying into the sea and backed them up to marshes that gave dangerous mosquitoes a breeding place. What might have been fertile plains had become swamps.

But the Jews had the heart to transform the land. They drained the swamps and prepared the soil for settlement. Some Jews purchased farms from the Arabs and some even employed Arabs to assist with the work. Others, either by themselves or in

Along with Israel's early agricultural transformation, there was a growing industry in taking potash from the Dead Sea.

communities, leased land from the Jewish National Fund's purchase of large holdings. The Histadrut was organized. More than a labor union, it trained immigrants to work the land and organized cooperatives for irrigation, transport, marketing, and even health and education.

While this transformation in agriculture was going on, many Jews were flocking to the cities. Tel Aviv had a population of one thousand in 1917, but by 1927 it had grown larger than Jerusalem. Jerusalem was growing beyond Old Jerusalem, and New Jerusalem was rapidly expanding. The harbor at Haifa was modernized. The Jordan River was utilized to give power to growing industries. Even on the desert there was a growing industry in taking potash and salt from the Dead Sea, the saltiest sea on earth.

By 1928 there were journals in the Hebrew language and a Hebrew theater, university, and technical institutes. Funds came from abroad to help found the schools and purchase land. From Russia, Poland, and Galicia Jews were rushing to Zion. Many of the immigrants were middle-class people accustomed to trade and commerce. Some were versed in high finance.

Israeli girls at army training camp

THE PALESTINE PROBLEM

As Jewish immigrants flooded into Palestine in the 1920s and 1930s, tensions arose between them and the Palestinian Arabs. The British, who had been assigned to facilitate a transition to independence, were faced with a problem. In the Balfour Declaration they had announced that they favored a Jewish national home in Palestine. But they had also said that nothing would be done that would compromise the civil and religious rights of existing non-Jewish communities. The influx of Jewish immigrants threatened to endanger the Arabs' civil rights.

In the 1930s, the Nazis' large-scale persecutions and executions of Jews spilled over into much of Eastern Europe. As a result, even greater numbers of Jewish refugees poured into Palestine, further endangering Arab-Jewish relations. Finally the British felt they had no choice but to limit Jewish immigration. In 1939 they issued

After the Nazis executed six million European Jews during World War II, hundreds of thousands of survivors hoped to relocate in the Promised Land. Among them were these refugees on the Exodus. *The British turned them away, feeling that further large-scale immigration would endanger relations between Arabs and Jews in Palestine.*

a White Paper, holding Jewish immigrants to ten thousand a year for five years, with no immigration after that. Needless to say, the Jewish community strongly opposed these restrictions.

Jewish soldiers fought side by side with the Allied soldiers during World War II, but when the war ended, Britain, recognizing the feelings of the Arabs, continued its restrictions on Jewish immigration. United States President Harry Truman called in vain for a lessening of the restrictions. In 1945 he asked the British to allow at least 100,000 European Jews who had been displaced during the war to settle in Palestine. The British would not agree to this.

Jews, meanwhile, were trying to immigrate regardless of restrictions. In the summer of 1947 the *Exodus*, carrying 4,515 refugees, reached the shores of Palestine. No one was allowed to land. The Promised Land was in sight, but the ship was ordered to turn back. The refugees were removed and put on transports to

Among the statues on the grounds of Yad Vashem in Jerusalem, where the victims of the Nazi Holocaust are memorialized, are the Warsaw Ghetto Memorial (left) and "The Silent Cry" (right).

France. France refused to let them land unless they did so willingly. But the Jews had had their sights set on Palestine ever since the trauma of European annihilation camps. Eventually, the ship went on to Hamburg, West Germany, and the Jews were forcibly removed. Newsreels showed the refugees being treated like nonpersons, and viewers in Europe and the United States were angry about Great Britain's restrictions.

In 1947 the United Nations partitioned Palestine into a Jewish state and an Arab state. Jerusalem was to be internationalized since it was the holy city of three faiths. The period for Great

Britain's mandate over Palestine came to an end the following year, and the British high commissioner left the country.

On the very day that the British high commissioner sailed from Haifa, May 14, 1948, the Israelis held a solemn ceremony in the Tel Aviv Museum of Art. *Hatikvah*, the national anthem, was sung, then David Ben-Gurion read the new Israeli Declaration of Independence.

In setting its borders according to United Nations guidelines, Israel was giving up more than half of the arable land on the west side of the Jordan, as well as many traditional and holy sites, but still the Arabs opposed the partition.

Egypt, Lebanon, and Syria moved restlessly on their borders. The day after the declaration was read and the council had approved a provisional government, the League of Arab States declared that it would seek to restore all of the land to the Palestinian Arabs. The armies of Egypt, Syria, Lebanon, Jordan, and Iraq, mostly with British arms, moved on the new state and invaded it from three sides. With a population of only some 650,000 Jews and a motley assortment of mostly obsolete weapons, Israel faced the Arab states. The Israeli army took Jaffa, drove the Arabs from Galilee, established a corridor from the Mediterranean to Jerusalem on the east, and forced the Egyptians out of most of the Negev. The Israelis were in control of about half the land the UN had designated for the Arabs, as well as the western half of Jerusalem. Jordan kept the West Bank, and Egypt the so-called Gaza Strip on the Mediterranean.

Ralph Bunche, a United States citizen, had been named mediator by the United Nations. He persuaded Egypt to sign an armistice in 1949. Jordan and Lebanon signed also. In July Syria signed.

The United States hastened to recognize the State of Israel. A year later Great Britain did the same.

Israel's permanent government was organized in early 1949. It was to be a democracy much like that of Great Britain. The parliament, called the Knesset, would have 120 members chosen at open polls. By the middle of February 1949, the Knesset had met, decided on its powers, and named David Ben-Gurion prime minister and Chaim Weizmann president. They decided not to have a written constitution, but adopted instead a series of basic laws that would eventually form chapters of a written constitution.

On May 11, 1949, Israel became a member of the United Nations. Immigrants began to flock in once again. These immigrants had to live in camps and be fed and clothed at government expense. The world Zionist organization was given the work of finding a place for all the newcomers. The newcomers set to work at once to learn Hebrew so that they could communicate with others. Germany, with the Nazi government out of power and now a democratic society, agreed to pay reparations to the Jews for losses suffered during the Holocaust.

DIFFICULT NEIGHBORS

Israel was not to have time to turn its full attention to internal affairs. In the mid-1950s Egypt continued blocking Israeli ships from using the Suez Canal. Israel turned to its port at Eilat on the Gulf of Aqaba as its only outlet for shipping to East Africa and Asia. But Egypt soon blocked Israeli ships there, too.

In October 1956 Israel invaded Egypt. Britain and France were engaged in the conflict as well. The Israelis went on to occupy the

Israeli artillery in action in Egypt and Syria during the Six-Day War

Gaza Strip and the Sinai Peninsula, but the UN, after arranging a cease-fire, sent troops to patrol these areas. The Gulf of Aqaba, at least, was opened again.

THE SIX-DAY WAR

Border clashes increased throughout the 1960s, until in May 1967 Egypt once again threatened Israel and blocked the Gulf of Aqaba. Israel's retaliation was swift and severe. On June 5, the Israeli air force destroyed the Egyptian air force. Jordan entered the war that same day. By June 8 Israeli troops occupied the Sinai Peninsula, the Gaza Strip, and the West Bank of the Jordan River, including east Jerusalem. By June 10 they had taken the Golan Heights on the Syrian border. In six days, Israel had occupied an area three times its own size.

THE YOM KIPPUR WAR

The explosive tensions between the Arabs and the Israelis were a matter of worldwide concern. After the Six-Day War both the UN and the United States proposed various resolutions to bring about

Egyptian President Anwar el-Sadat (left), United States President Jimmy Carter (center), and Israeli Prime Minister Menachem Begin (right) face the press at the conclusion of the Camp David Accords of 1978.

a compromise, if not a lasting peace, in the Middle East. But peace was not to be. On October 6, 1973, on the Jewish holy day of Yom Kippur (the Day of Atonement), the Arabs staged an attack. With Egypt penetrating the Sinai Peninsula and Syria moving on the Golan Heights, Israel was engaged in vicious battles on two fronts.

Though the UN once again arranged a cease-fire, the prospect of peace did not begin to appear until late 1977, when Israeli Prime Minister Menachem Begin and Egyptian President Anwar el-Sadat met to discuss a settlement of their nations' long-standing enmity. The Camp David Accords of 1978, arranged by United States President Jimmy Carter, were a major step. Both leaders agreed to sign a peace treaty. Israel agreed to withdraw from the Sinai Peninsula. It also agreed to allow the Gaza Strip and the West Bank to govern themselves (although this was never set up). Egypt agreed to peace and to the establishment of diplomatic relations with Israel. This peace treaty was signed in 1979.

AFTER CAMP DAVID

Relations between Israel and Egypt improved after the Egypt-Israel Peace Treaty. However, tense relations continued with other Arab nations who felt that the treaty overlooked Arabs' interests. The most persistent threat came from the Palestine Liberation Organization (PLO), a group representing Palestinian Arabs who want a separate Palestinian state. Hoping to stop PLO terrorist attacks, Israeli troops invaded Lebanon in 1982, attacking PLO bases and moving north to occupy PLO headquarters in West Beirut. The Israelis finally withdrew in 1985, leaving Lebanon with heavy civilian casualties and Israel with a damaged reputation.

Meanwhile, Israel's 1984 elections resulted in the formation of a unity government. Under this plan, Labor party leader Shimon Peres and Likud party head Yitzhak Shamir would each serve as prime minister for two years.

GOVERNMENT

In Israel every person over eighteen may vote in an open election. There are many political parties. The Knesset, Israel's parliament, has 120 members, elected for four-year terms. The men and women who are elected meet in the elegant Knesset building. They sit with other members of their political party and face the horseshoe-shaped seating section that the cabinet members occupy.

The Knesset selects the president, who is the head of state, for a five-year term of office. Being the president is a high honor, although the office holds little power. The president, for instance,

The Knesset, Israel's elegant parliament building

attends state dinners and ground-breaking ceremonies. The important position is that of prime minister, who is chosen by the party in power and can be either a man or a woman. The prime minister is the head of government and selects the cabinet. Any time that the Knesset loses confidence in the prime minister, he or she has to call a new election. Because there are more than two parties, no one party ever has the majority of the votes. The prime minister has to depend on the votes of smaller parties that form a coalition. In this way even small parties have a voice in policymaking.

Menachem Begin was prime minister from 1977 to 1983. When he resigned, Yitzhak Shamir took his place. In September 1984, by agreement between parties, Shimon Peres became prime minister; he was to serve until October 1986, when Shamir would hold the office for the following twenty-five months.

Civil and religious courts serve the three communities: Jewish, Christian, and Muslim. Civil courts handle crime. Religious courts have charge of marriage and divorce, for example. The Histadrut oversees health and welfare, commercial enterprises, and labor.

Israel's kibbutzim are communities whose members work for the kibbutz and share equally in the results of their labors. All members receive food, housing, clothing, education, and medical care in return for their contribution to the community. The woman above is selecting clothes for her family in a kibbutz shop. The kibbutz shown below is in the Galilee.

Chapter 4
KIBBUTZ LIVING

In 1909 a group of young Jews left their homes in Russia to make new homes in the Holy Land. They wanted to farm and at the same time try a social experiment: a community where everything was shared by its members. A place where money or position was not a measure of a person's worth—that was their dream. And what a land they found!

The land, neglected for centuries, was not fit for agriculture. There were swamps, winter rains had carried off topsoil, sand swirled over the desert, there was no irrigation. To people with less zeal the land would have seemed worthless. But these young pioneers knew something of modern farming. They knew that much of the land could be rehabilitated. The first move was to drain the swamps that covered much of the richest soil; the next, to control the erosion by harnessing the winter rains. Even the dunes were anchored so they would not invade cultivated land.

Of course, this first group of farmers couldn't do all of this. As the land called to its people, more and more workers came to what was then Palestine.

The chief problem was irrigation. The pioneers drilled wells and maintained storage reservoirs so little rainwater was lost. They established sewage reclamation projects, built piping systems, improved brackish water, and worked on taking the salt from seawater.

Reclaiming land is a slow process. By 1948 there were 400,000 acres (161,874 hectares) under cultivation. In the next twenty years that amount was more than doubled. In 1979, 1.1 million acres (445,150 hectares) were producing crops. Among all of the people was the contagious feeling that there was work to be done.

THE KIBBUTZ

So the dream of successful farming came true. What about the dream of a community where all were equal and shared equally in the result of their labors? This dream was fulfilled in the kibbutzim. ("Kibbutzim" is the plural form of "kibbutz.") The 1909 group of Russian immigrants built the first kibbutz south of the Sea of Galilee and laid the foundation for what is now Degania Kibbutz. As this kibbutz succeeded, others were developed.

The Degania Kibbutz was begun on a site that commanded the approach to Galilee and Haifa. It was built stone by stone. The motto of the residents, called kibbutzniks, was "Work and Believe." Less than a mile from the Syrian frontier, they built a pleasant village surrounded by cypress and eucalyptus trees. There were orchards of fruit and rich gardens. When the Syrians attacked, the kibbutzniks defended their homes against trained artillery and tanks with a collection of outmoded rifles—and won!

There are kibbutzniks who no longer lead an austere life but

The Degania Kibbutz, built by a group of Russian Jews who arrived in 1909, was the first such community in what is now Israel.

live comfortably. There are still poor kibbutzim where life is a struggle. No matter how comfortable or how austere living is, the kibbutzniks use the same system of government.

The kibbutz is governed by committees. Each committee is responsible for a phase of the community life: economic planning, finance, education, culture, care of children, for example. Once a year there is a special meeting. The policies for the next year are formulated for the entire group, officers are elected, and disagreements are discussed and solved by the complete membership. No one is tied to the kibbutz. Members can transfer to another kibbutz or move to independent farms or into crafts or trades. The people who live in the kibbutzim live there because they want to.

Women work just as the men do. In order to free women from responsibility at home, everyone eats at a common table. The kibbutz House of Children is a children's paradise. No other method of child rearing equals it for education and fun. In some kibbutzim the children live day and night in the House of Children, spending only a few hours a day with their parents. Now in many kibbutzim the children sleep in their parents' home at night, and a closer bonding between parents and children is developed.

At first all kibbutzim were engaged in agriculture. As artisans as well as farmers formed kibbutzim, entire groups turned to other industries. Now a given kibbutz might blow glass or make toys, furniture, shoes, or even electronic equipment.

Some kibbutzim have modern kitchens, swimming pools, and gymnasiums. Others have art galleries, concert halls, and cultural centers. Cultural facilities are often shared with neighboring villages. Kibbutzim may even operate tourist facilities or make arrangements for young people from other countries to share the life of the kibbutz.

No matter how plain or how luxurious, everything that is owned, produced, and earned is shared equally by members of the community. There is real equality—equality of opportunity and of responsibility. But kibbutzniks aren't all alike. One of their freedoms is to be themselves. They don't wear uniforms, nor do they all behave alike.

Yet, successful as the kibbutz is, less than 4 percent of the people of Israel live in kibbutzim. Other people look up to kibbutzniks as something special, for they are almost alone in being responsible for Israel's successful scientific farming. Some members of the Knesset, Israel's governing body, come from kibbutzim. A cabinet member may serve table or work in the dairy when he isn't solving international or national problems.

THE MOSHAV

There are some village people who prefer to make their own decisions, cook in their own kitchens, and eat at their own tables. These families live in a moshav (plural: "moshavim"). The moshav is also a cooperative, but with more independence for the people, though they stay within national and regional planning. Each family owns several acres of farmland. Cooperation works to their advantage. Purchasing and selling are both done cooperatively.

Although Kiryat-Gat is not on any main road and has no religious shrines to attract tourists, it is regularly visited by interested foreigners who want to see just how a moshav town works. There are a number of villages grouped around a central town. The town collects and distributes the produce and furnishes raw materials, equipment, and tools. It is the administrative center. This may be a model for individual farming in the future.

How does Israel assure that the people in kibbutzim and moshavim have cultural opportunities? In the central town around which the villages are grouped there is a secondary school, a concert hall, a theater, and classes in cultural subjects for adults. The fine things in life are within the reach of everyone.

It is the dedicated, pioneer spirit that has made the desert "blossom as a rose" in Israel.

The Russian Orthodox Church of St. Mary Magdalene on the Mount of Olives overlooks the holy city of Jerusalem.

Chapter 5

CITIES, THE OLD AND THE NEW

While it was the inspired farmers who began the "ascent to the land," more than 70 percent of Israelis live in cities and towns. Some have their homes in great cities such as Jerusalem, Tel Aviv, and Haifa. Others live in smaller cities from Dan in upper Galilee to Eilat on the Gulf of Aqaba.

JERUSALEM

Jerusalem has been called by many the most interesting city in the world. Surely it is one of the most important. It is a holy city to three great religions. It has lived, if not always in stone and mortar, in the hearts of the Jews for five thousand years, in Christian hearts for almost two thousand, and it has been a holy city of Islam for some fourteen hundred years.

Twenty-five times Jerusalem has changed hands. What other city has suffered as much and survived?

We look at Old Jerusalem, think of its past, and say, "How very small it is!" The old city wall that was built by Suleiman the Magnificent in the 1500s is only two and a half miles (four kilometers) long. One could jog the whole circumference in twenty minutes! In this wall are eight gates, all of them important in the city's history.

Old Jerusalem was divided into five parts. Four were living quarters for Muslims, Christians, Jews, and Armenians. The fifth part is the Temple Mount where once the Jewish temple with its Holy of Holies stood. Now one of the most beautiful buildings in the world is there: the Dome of the Rock, a Muslim shrine. Under the dome is the historic Moriah Rock. It is to this rock that Abraham brought his son Isaac to sacrifice him to God. The rock was later incorporated into Solomon's Temple, where burnt offerings were made upon it.

The Muslims also have reason for holding it sacred. Muhammad was said to have dreamed while he was hidden in a cave in Arabia that, accompanied by an angel, he rode through the skies on the back of his miraculous steed from Arabia to Jerusalem. From the Moriah Rock he ascended through seven heavens to the presence of Allah.

The mosque built over the rock is of beautiful mosaic. There are tall stained-glass windows with words from the Koran inscribed above them in tiled Arabic letters. The dome shines like gold. Worshipers can pray as individuals in the Dome of the Rock, but Friday group worship is in a mosque, El Aqsa, at the southern end of the temple esplanade facing Mecca. From the minarets of this mosque the faithful are called to prayer five times a day.

Above: One of the eight gates in the old city wall of Jerusalem
Below: This view of Old Jerusalem captures the character of the city.

Mediter ranean Sea

Tel Aviv-
Jaffa

Jerusalem

Dead
Sea

Some Christians believe that the Garden Tomb is the place where Christ was buried.

The Church of the Holy Sepulcher is one of the holiest sanctuaries in Christendom. It is built on the traditional place where Christ died, was buried, and rose from the dead. The church is shared by six religious groups, each of which has its own sections: Greek Orthodox, Roman Catholic, Coptic, Armenian, Syrian, and Abyssinian. These sects share the major rights to the basilica, but any Christian can worship there.

In the center of the rotunda is a marble sepulcher where, according to tradition, Jesus was wrapped in his burial clothes.

Just through the Damascus Gate is a quiet, green garden, the Garden Tomb. Some Christians believe that this quiet hillock is

In Old Jerusalem, site of a weekly Arab livestock market (above), there are vaulted, covered bazaars, crowded market alleys, and handicraft workshops (left).

the authentic place where Christ died and was buried.

In 1948 there were 1,800 Jews living and studying in the Jewish quarter of the Old City. Near the Western Wall, or Wailing Wall, there were fifty-eight synagogues, religious schools, and academies. In the Muslim Quarter were 2,500 Arabs. The Arabs controlled the tourist trade. There have been Christian pilgrims to Jerusalem ever since the Byzantine period.

The center of Old Jerusalem has vaulted, covered bazaars and crowded market alleys. From the bazaars and alleys, steps instead of streets climb the steep hills to the living quarters. The bazaars and markets are crowded, noisy, colorful, and fragrant with baking bread, sizzling meat, and exotic fruits.

Old Jerusalem (above) presents a striking contrast to New Jerusalem (opposite page).

NEW JERUSALEM

In the bazaars, the markets, and the crowded residential quarters of the walled city, one recognizes the sights and sounds of the Middle East. It is a special Middle East. The clothing is unlike that of Syria or Saudi Arabia, for example. Nowhere else can one see the flat black hats and the neat ringlets in front of the ears of Orthodox Jewish men and boys. Even though tourists from Europe and America are being led or shepherded everywhere by tourist guides, one can imagine pilgrims of another and distant past looking at the ornate shrines and the sacred churches, mosques, and synagogues.

The Israelis are building modern housing developments to the north of Jerusalem as the city continues to expand.

But when one leaves Old Jerusalem, the feeling of being in a time-tied city is lost. New Jerusalem is a city so shining, so new, so understated in its elegance that one seems to have been transferred to another world—a world not necessarily better, nor even more beautiful, but definitely different.

Easily the most commanding building is the Knesset, the home of Israel's legislative body. The four-story building is square, the roof flat, supported by columns on the four sides. It is imposing and elegant in its simplicity. Beautiful sculptured iron gates open onto the Knesset Plaza, and a huge bronze menorah stands in front of the plaza. The menorah—a seven-branched candlestick, symbol of the State of Israel—was given to the Israeli parliament by the British parliament. On the side of the menorah that faces the Knesset are twenty-nine sculptured reliefs of important events in Israel's history. Between the Knesset and the menorah is an open space where demonstrators often protest various government actions.

Directly across from the Knesset and other government buildings is the new Hebrew University. In the troubled time between 1949 and 1967 when students couldn't get to the original Hebrew University on Mount Scopus, the government built on high ground a dazzling complex of university buildings on beautifully landscaped terraces. Each building houses a separate college, each has its own faculty. When the 1967 hostilities were over and Mount Scopus with its splendid view of the entire area was again open, the government remodeled and refurbished the university buildings there and built many new ones. Hebrew University now has two campuses, and enrollment is growing rapidly.

Not far away is the Valley of the Cross, a wooded ravine so named because tradition says that the wood for Christ's cross came from this place. Rising out of the valley is the huge Monastery of the Cross. This is a massive building, twice rebuilt, which displays priceless frescoes and mosaics. Above it is the recently built Israel Museum, a series of modern buildings including art pavilions, an archaeological wing, an open-air sculpture garden, and the Shrine of the Book. This is a museum devoted to the Dead Sea Scrolls, the most recently found—and oldest—manuscripts of the Old Testament in the Hebrew language. The scrolls were discovered in 1947 in a cave near the Dead Sea by a boy who was looking for a lost sheep.

The Shrine of the Book houses the Dead Sea Scrolls, the oldest manuscripts of the Old Testament in the Hebrew language.

New Jerusalem still has room to expand to the north. It can continue to grow and grow. The new portion of the city is prosperous and richly diverse. Ashkenazi Jews from eastern and central Europe; Sephardic Jews from Spain; others from the Mediterranean world, the Near and Middle East, Yemen, and Morocco—all have helped to make New Jerusalem a beautiful and thriving city.

There are attractive residential areas, busy commercial areas, thriving industrial complexes, and impressive public buildings. There are schools, clinics, shopping centers, hotels, swimming pools, gymnasiums, theaters, and a huge concert hall.

All of the buildings are built of Jerusalem stone, which gives the entire city unity, a special charm, a personality unlike any other city in the world.

In the modern city of Tel Aviv (above) it does not seem surprising to find avant-garde structures such as this new building (left).

TEL AVIV

Tel Aviv, like Jerusalem, is really two cities, the old and the new. The old is the ancient city of Jaffa (Yafo) which, according to tradition, was founded by Noah's son Japhet. It was from Jaffa that the legendary Jonah set sail, only to be swallowed by the whale. In Jaffa, at the house of Simon the Tanner, Christ's apostle Peter is said to have raised Tabitha from the dead, and announced that Christ's teachings were for the gentile as well as the Jew.

In 1909 a group of Jewish settlers started a suburb to the north of Jaffa. By 1948 the suburb had become a city and in 1950 it was united with Jaffa into one city. Now the Tel Aviv-Jaffa complex is Israel's second-largest metropolitan area, with over a million inhabitants. It is alive with business and unmatched any place in the world for culture.

This modern fountain (above) is the focal point of Dizengoff Square, which is surrounded by Tel Aviv's most fashionable shops. The city's busy marina (left) is on the eastern shore of the Mediterranean Sea.

The push of progress can be felt in the fine shopping areas, where one may window-shop or buy the latest fashions and the most modern appliances and furniture or where fine Yemenite handwork, filigree, metalwork, and hand-embroidered blouses and scarves are sold. There are beautiful diamonds, fine Persian carpets, and musical instruments. In a record shop one may buy today's music, the classics, or the folk songs of Israel.

There are parks and gardens for strolling. A beautiful fountain stands in the center of Dizengoff Square. In Kings of Israel Square lovely illuminated fountains give an otherworldly feeling. This square is frequently used for open-air concerts.

There are a busy marina and inside and outside swimming pools and gymnasiums for the health-conscious. The airport is near. Everything that a great city needs, Tel Aviv has.

The clock tower in the center of Old Jaffa (left), was built in 1906. Nearby is one of the city's many minarets. Jaffa's bustling main street (right) is lined with shops and advertisements.

But there is more: culture. The Habimah Theater, which was founded in Russia and is now Israel's national theater, is one of many theaters. There is the Zionist Center where Scripture readings can be heard and the songs and dances of Israeli peasants are appreciated. The Frederic Mann Auditorium is the home of the Israel Philharmonic Orchestra. The city is rich in museums. The Diaspora Museum is one of many. There are art museums and folklore museums. Tel Aviv University is famous for its scholarship.

But to feel the depth and richness of history, go to Jaffa. Here are open markets where one can haggle and bargain with real excitement. Along the byways of the old city are galleries that have been set up by artists. The twisting alleys that wander downhill to the harbor have been changed to artist quarters. Traditional food is served in quaint restaurants, and there are even nightclubs.

The Church of Saint Peter was built on the ruins of a medieval fortress in 1654. The beautiful Mahmudiye Mosque was built in 1810.

Between Tel Aviv and Haifa to the north, there are many small communities interspersed with farms and sand dunes. The sand dunes have a beauty of their own.

Tel Aviv has become a megalopolis, young and vitally alive. More than any other city on the Mediterranean coast, its mixture of old and new lends a feeling of excitement that makes it unique.

HAIFA

In 1905 Haifa, built on the slopes of Mount Carmel, was a little town of 10,000 people. Now it is Israel's third-largest city, with a population of almost 250,000. Why the tremendous growth? Israel's industrial boom is the explanation. Haifa has long been Israel's major Mediterranean port (although it is now rivaled by the newer port of Ashdod, south of Tel Aviv). East of Haifa near the mouth of the Qishon River there are oil refineries, all kinds of heavy industry, and great shipyards.

It is in the Bay of Haifa that the *Patria*, loaded with refugees, was blown up in the 1947 attempt to deport Jewish immigrants.

Haifa is a beautiful city in spite of its being an industrial center. Mount Carmel is always inspiring and Haifa has one of the most beautiful bays on the entire Mediterranean coast. It is a delightful place in which to live since it blends tradition with tomorrow.

Haifa is the world center of the Baha'i faith. The Baha'is believe that some day there will be one religion, one common language, and all men will be brothers. They accept all prophets as representing God, and their prophet, Baha-Ulla, is one of these.

The golden-domed Baha'i Shrine, set amid the beautiful Persian Gardens on the slopes of Mount Carmel, is the most impressive building in Haifa. Below the shrine, broad David Ben-Gurion Boulevard leads directly to the harbor.

Israel has accepted the Baha'is' freedom to worship. In Haifa, the Baha'is have built a shrine with a golden dome over the grave of their founder, Mirsa Ali Muhammad. Baha'i believers dream that this shrine will one day be the center of the unified church of the world.

These are the three great cities, but there are many others that are important as Christian shrines, especially interesting in history, unique to Israel, or examples of the country's special development.

BETHLEHEM

A few miles south of Jerusalem in the Judean hills, Bethlehem lies in a fertile valley. The nature of the valley is described by the city's name, which means "house of bread." To the east the wilderness of Judah falls to the Dead Sea.

Tradition and history envelop the town. The Old Testament's Ruth returned with her mother-in-law, Naomi, to Bethlehem, and

This is the view of Bethlehem from the Basilica of the Nativity, the church built on the spot where Jesus is thought to have been born.

it was in these fields that she met her second husband, Boaz. This was King David's hometown, near which he was herding sheep when his father sent him to check on his brothers who were fighting the Philistines, and he ended by killing Goliath. Rachel died at the birth of her second son, Benjamin, and was buried here.

Joseph and Mary, being of the House of David, came to Bethlehem for a census, and Jesus was born in a manger there. In A.D. 325 Constantine built a church over the grotto where the birth supposedly took place, and Justinian replaced it in the sixth century with the basilica that still stands today. Thousands of Christians visit the Basilica of the Nativity every year, and on Christmas Eve at midnight a Christmas high mass is celebrated.

The town is half Christian and half Muslim now, and it has changed hands almost as often as Jerusalem. It was controlled by Romans, Byzantines, Arabs, Crusaders, Mamelukes, and Turks before becoming an important town in the contested West Bank.

Capernaum
Sea of Galilee
Nazareth
Mediterranean Sea
Jericho
Hebron

NAZARETH

In a circle of cypress-covered hills is the city of Nazareth. It is
an Arab city; some of the Arabs are Muslim and some are
Christian. The town looks tired and shabby, but behind it a new
city is rising. This town, too, is dominated by shrines. The Church
of St. Joseph stands where Joseph's carpentry shop is thought to
have stood. Mary's Well is marked. But most beautiful and ornate
is the Basilica of the Annunciation. The present basilica is the fifth
church to stand on the site of Mary's house, called the Grotto of
the Annunciation.

CAPERNAUM

Capernaum is a city especially dear to Christian pilgrims
because Christ is said to have done much of his teaching there. It
was in Capernaum that Christ first found his apostles James, John,
Simon, and Andrew fishing. The Octagon of St. Peter is an
octagonal church built over St. Peter's house. The small house,
dating back to the first century A.D., contains inscriptions
mentioning the names of Jesus and Peter, as well as a number of
fishing hooks.

JERICHO

Just north of the Dead Sea is the oldest city in the world,
Jericho. Still remaining is part of a stone tower built about
8000 B.C. How does a town exist in the Judean desert? Jericho is
built on an oasis with water from a natural spring.

When the Israelites returned from Egypt they crossed the Jordan

The Dead Sea Scrolls were discovered in the hills of Qumran (left), a few miles south of Jericho.
There is still a street of carpenter shops in Nazareth (right), where Jesus, the son of a carpenter, grew up.

and conquered Jericho. Christians believe that John baptized Christ near here. The Christian shrines that have been built by worshipers dominate the town.

Near Jericho are the Mount of Temptation, where Jesus fasted for forty days, and the Greek Monastery of St. John. A few miles south of the mount, on the naked hills of Qumran, the Dead Sea Scrolls were found in a cave.

HEBRON

Hebron may be the oldest unwalled city in the world that has been lived in continuously. In 1700 B.C. it was King David's capital.

Now it boasts a thriving glass industry. Glassmaking is an art as old as history. The Phoenicians made beautiful glass, and when the Crusaders came they took the art back to Europe. Many of the returning Crusaders settled in Venice and developed Venetian glass. Italian Jews, fleeing the Inquisition, took the glassmaking art back to Israel. They settled in Hebron. So the art that could have been transferred 100 miles (161 kilometers) was taken from Acre to Venice and back again to make Hebron a glassblowing center.

Although this is an important industry, it is usually a family enterprise, with all of the family participating and the craft being passed from the father to the children.

The principal shrine in Hebron is the Tomb of the Patriarchs, which stands above the Machpelah Cave. Three Biblical couples, Abraham and Sarah, Isaac and Rebecca, and Jacob and Leah are buried there. (Some people say that Adam and Eve are buried here, too.) To the Muslims these men and women are sacred, and they have erected near the tomb the Mosque of Ibrahim (Abraham). Across from the mosque stands a synagogue. This shrine is the only one in Israel where Jews and Muslims worship together.

CAESAREA

Caesarea is a magnificent harbor city. Its present claim to fame is that it has the only golf course and club in all of Israel. There are elegant homes and a five-star hotel.

But what really makes it important is that Herod built a small city here in 22 B.C. Still standing, and used for open air concerts and other cultural events, is a Roman amphitheater. Herod's city is in ruins but it recalls the preaching of Peter and Paul. Archaeologists have uncovered a stone slab inscribed with the name of Pontius Pilate, who was governor here from A.D. 26 to 36.

ACRE

Acre was the most important port on this part of the Mediterranean coast when the Phoenicians were daring, far-traveling seagoers who are thought by some historians to have reached as far as Mexico. When the Crusaders came to the Holy Land with the goal of taking it from the Turks, Acre was the Crusader capital. The dining hall of the Knights Hospitalers of St. John of Jerusalem is in the underground Crusader city.

Now that Tel Aviv and Haifa are great ports, Acre is the anchorage for the fishing fleet. There is a beautiful beach at Acre with shallow, calm water and a wide stretch of fine, sun-kissed sand. Thousands of bathers and swimmers enjoy it.

From a distance the walls and battlements built by the Turks, the white minarets, the fishing boats, and the blue sea make Acre seem like a storybook city.

BEERSHEBA

Not too long ago Beersheba was a tired, dusty, sun-baked town. Now it is an example of what energy and modern know-how can do to modernize a city under very difficult circumstances.

In today's Beersheba there is a university named for David Ben-Gurion, who dreamed and worked to awaken the Negev Desert. The city is a modern university town and the "capital of Negev." Here are the Arid Zone Research Institute, a modern hospital, and a medical school. An archaeological and ethnic museum is a reminder of Bible days when Beersheba was an important point on the ancient route between Jerusalem and Egypt.

Every Thursday there is a Bedouin market. The noisy trade is

Sheep, goats, and camels are traded at the regular Thursday morning Bedouin market in Beersheba. Bedouin women wear the traditional black robes and keep their faces covered.

largely in sheep, goats, and camels. The women, dressed in traditional black and often with children hanging to their robes, drive the herds with skill. Part of the interest in Beersheba is the contrast between city people, living in the modern housing units built to minimize the intolerable summer heat, and the Bedouin families not far away, living in tents as they have since the earliest times.

In Beersheba the new seems to dominate the old, though sheep sometimes still graze in front of the university.

EILAT

The western border of the northern half of Israel is on the Mediterranean Sea. Tel Aviv and Haifa have excellent ports that are open to goods from the West. But Eilat is on the Gulf of Aqaba, which leads to the Red Sea and opens trade to East Africa and the

Eilat (left) with its beaches, hotels, restaurants, and nightclubs, has become an important winter vacation resort. Located at the very tip of the Negev Desert on the Gulf of Aqaba, which extends north from the Red Sea (right), it is Israel's southernmost town.

Orient. Eilat is a beautiful town on the very tip of the Negev. It is near the copper mines that Solomon utilized and that functioned again until the mid-1970s. Eilat is a great tourist center, too. There are new hotels, entertainment, excitement. One can reach it by private car, by bus, by plane, and on its warm, beautiful beaches have a holiday.

The Red Sea itself is beautiful beyond imagination. Beneath the waters are coral reefs in a variety of patterns and colors, sea anemones, and tropical fish of every brilliant hue.

Continuing west into the Sinai from Eilat, traveling into an area now controlled by Egypt, are the magnificent mountains where Moses is said to have received the Ten Commandments. The sea along the coast is yellow-brown, purple, azure, sapphire, and violet.

What splendor, what heart-lifting beauty.

The Israelis, in their continuing attempts to reclaim land for crops (above),
are expanding the National Water Carrier, a complex irrigation
system that brings water from the Sea of Galilee to the Negev Desert (below).

Chapter 6

WORKING

When any nation desires to be self-reliant, one of its major activities must be farming. People must eat, and producing food must be a basic responsibility.

The young Jews who made their first "ascent to the land," the first *aliyah*, didn't find rich farmland. There were patches that had been farmed, but most of the land had been abused and neglected for centuries. When they drained the marshes they found that there was rich farmland waiting to be reclaimed. In other areas the flash downpours of seasonal rain had washed away the topsoil and there was little left to nourish any plants. Farms were made by dragging out the rocks and uncovering the soil. Many farms were walled with the stones that were removed. There were areas where the soil was good but there was no water. Water conservation and irrigation were necessary.

It is amazing, almost a miracle, that in a country whose arable area is as small as Israel's (only 20 percent of the total land area) so much food and cotton can be produced. Of course the organization of the kibbutz and the moshav account for a great deal of the success of farming. But scientists deserve credit, too. These experts have experimented and researched and have made themselves the most enlightened in the world. They have taught the farmers to farm intensively, and the farmers have been willing to learn to get the most from every acre of land. Many countries of the Near and Middle East have been limited by lack of advanced methods and the feeling that familiar ways are best. The forward-looking Israelis have expertise and a social and political organization that makes it possible for them to use all that they are discovering in their careful study.

For example, they have built the National Water Carrier, a complex irrigation system that brings water from the Sea of Galilee to the Negev Desert. They have also devised "plastic farming," a system of plastic coverings over crops that creates a mini-greenhouse in the fields.

The most common crops are grain, cotton, vegetables, and grapes. Because of the diversity of climate oranges, bananas, and dates are also grown. Farming is a respected profession.

MORE GIFTS FROM THE EARTH

While food is, of course, the most important product to any country, food is not enough. Any nation that has to buy products from abroad must have something to sell abroad. Otherwise all the money would go one way—out.

The Israelis looked to the earth for other gifts: minerals. In the south there are huge, rust-colored columns of sandstone that guard Solomon's Mines. At the time of Solomon, copper was the metal of kings. It may have been copper from those very mines, crafted into swords, spears, and shields, that made Solomon's mighty kingdom possible. Heaps of black slag still mark the place of Solomon's smelters.

Huge, rust-colored pillars of sandstone (left) mark the location of King Solomon's ancient copper mines near Timna. Columns of rock salt (right) are scattered on the shore of the Dead Sea, which produces a wealth of minerals even more important to Israel than copper.

But more important than the copper, even more exportable, are the minerals that come from the Dead Sea. Some of these are magnesium, sodium, calcium, potassium, potash, and bromides.

Huge salt pans on the Dead Sea enable the water to evaporate quickly, leaving potassium salts behind. Workers then shovel up chunks of salt from the bottom of the shallow pans.

Even the desert makes a contribution. On the central plains of the Negev phosphates are found, and in the south near Eilat, granite is quarried. Near Beersheba, queen city of the desert, there are the materials to make glass, ceramics, tile, and even fine porcelain.

Fishing and diamond cutting are two of Israel's most important industries. These fishermen (left) are repairing their nets in the harbor at Acre. The man above is inspecting finished diamonds.

GIFTS FROM THE SEA

One of the major industries of Israel is fishing, though there aren't many fish in the Sea of Galilee or along the Mediterranean coast. The fishing boats go all the way to the Ethiopian coast. A fleet of more than five hundred fishing boats harbors at Acre.

In addition to the fish brought in by the fleet, fish farming in the north of Israel and in inland ponds is becoming a popular kind of farming. The fish supply the needs of Israel and are exported, making fishing rank with agriculture as a major source of income.

LABOR AND MANUFACTURING

Israel has a very special labor union, the General Federation of Labor, or Histadrut. Eighty percent of the adults in Israel belong to this organization. It is not a labor union like those in most nations because it owns many of Israel's businesses. Before 1949 it encouraged immigration and helped find homes and jobs for immigrants.

Now the Histadrut has three divisions: a union of laborers, a commission to develop industrial and commercial projects, and another to take charge of health and welfare. The entire organization of the Histadrut has many responsibilities. Every member of the Israeli cabinet belongs to the Histadrut. Founded in 1920, it is the organization that can be praised for guiding Israel's remarkable progress.

The Vulcan Steel Foundries produce steel for aircraft, armaments, and other industry. The aircraft industry is growing most rapidly. Israel has had to put so much into self-preservation that planes and arms have had to come first. Automobiles are assembled in Israel but are not yet produced there.

The textile industry is one of the largest industries in Israel. Thousands of men and women are employed at textile mills making some of the finest fabrics in the world. As in farming, science should get some of the credit. Sophisticated electric controls supplement human power.

There is a related industry, that of producing fine garments. Israel produces much high-fashion clothing, including swimwear and leather clothing. Much of this is done in cottages and villages so each garment is an individual work of art.

Although diamonds are not produced in Israel, diamond cutting, polishing, and trading are important occupations. The Israeli diamond market is the largest in the world. About half the gemstone diamonds sold today are cut in Israel.

Raw products that are produced in Israel and many that are imported are used in the active manufacturing industry. Farm products are turned into finished food, beverages, and especially wine. These are consumed at home but there is a surplus for export. Steel is manufactured into sophisticated machinery for

Because Israel is short of coal and oil resources, solar energy has become an important source of power for homes in the south (left). A huge oil refinery in Haifa uses imported oil, and the country's factories produce an amazing variety of products, including steel, glass, and chemicals (right).

other industries. Natural materials are made into ceramics, tile, and especially glass. There are rubber goods, plastics, fine leather products, paper, and cardboard.

Almost anything produced elsewhere can be produced in Israel. There is no shortage of well-trained personnel. Devising better methods of production is a part of the entire scheme. For instance, although Israel's oil and coal resources are not significant, solar energy has been developed extensively as a source of power.

All of this almost volcanic development has taken capital, which the government has supplied in the form of loans. This—with welfare needed for new immigrants and the planes and arms needed because of the troubled Middle East—forced inflation as high as 400 percent in 1984, although it is now well under 50 percent.

Camels are a favorite mode of transport for Israel's Bedouins (left). The country's extensive road system, which continues to expand (right), makes it possible to travel by automobile or bus to nearly any place in the country.

TRANSPORTATION

A young Israeli man remembers having walked 26 miles (42 kilometers) to visit his cousin. But perhaps he didn't walk all the way. Hitchhiking is commonplace. Private automobiles are discouraged because they still must be imported, so the government prefers to maintain inexpensive travel. There is a choice of bus, train, or plane. The train runs from Nahariyya near the Lebanese border to Beersheba in the Negev, between Tel Aviv and Gaza, and between Jerusalem and Tel Aviv. There are more than 2,500 miles (4,023 kilometers) of paved highways, which makes bus travel to nearly any place possible.

Arkia (Israel Inland Airlines) operates daily flights between cities in Israel. The national airline, El Al, flies to major cities around the world.

Of course, there are still donkeys and, on the Negev, camels.

Though most holidays observed in Israel are religious, Independence Day (above)
is a secular celebration. Christians celebrate Easter with a procession
down the Via Dolorosa (below left), and Muslims (below right) observe
Ramadan with a month of fasting.

Chapter 7

HOLIDAYS

The people of Israel are unusually hard workers. They have ambition not only for themselves but also for their land. Do they ever take holidays? They love holidays! Because Jerusalem is sacred to Jews, Christians, and Muslims, the calendar is filled with holidays, mostly of religious significance.

JEWISH HOLIDAYS

Jewish holidays are dated according to the Jewish calendar. Many Jewish calendars since 1948 have included Israel Independence Day in May, marking the end of the Jews' nineteen hundred years of exile. It is a gala day that differs from religious holidays in that it is more political, like Bastille Day in France or the Fourth of July in the United States. The day begins with a celebration at the tomb of Theodor Herzl, father of Zionism. This ceremony is followed by dancing in the streets and general celebrating.

The Jewish New Year usually falls in September. Rosh Hashanah isn't a noisy, hilarious welcoming in of a new year. It is rather a serious look at the past. It begins a ten-day period of recollection and repentance. The climax of the ten days of repentance is Yom Kippur, the holiest day of the year. This is also called the Day of Atonement.

The Yom Kippur service begins with the Kol Nidre chant. This stirring, haunting melody pleads for God to absolve the faithful from solemn vows to safeguard against accidental violations.

When the evening service is over some people stay in the synagogue all night and all the next day until sunset. Some go home but continue to fast and pray and return the next day to continue praying and meditating. They meditate on who they are, what their life has been, what their life can be in the future. Atonement must include making peace not only with God but also with one's fellowmen.

A climactic moment of the Yom Kippur morning service is reached when the rabbi stands before the ark, about to remove the scrolls, and prays to God in the words of Moses. At the end of Yom Kippur, the Day of Atonement, the ram's horn, or *shofar*, is blown, filling the worshipers with a sense of exaltation.

Sukkot comes only eight days after the Day of Atonement. It is really a harvest festival, but it has a historical background.

When Moses and his sometimes unwilling followers set out from Egypt to go to the Promised Land, they didn't know that the journey would take a long, long time. Two generations would be spent in the wilderness. They didn't travel every day; rather they returned to the nomadic ways of their forefathers and stopped for a time whenever they came upon an oasis that offered vegetation and water. When they paused for a time they built temporary shelters or booths. Sometimes these were of clay, sometimes of sticks and brush, sometimes tents of animal skins. These are the booths that are celebrated in Sukkot.

Now in Jewish centers Jews often build booths of material that is convenient to them and decorate them with fruits and vegetables. In Jewish temples everywhere there are services of

The Kibbutz Shefayim celebrates Hanukkah with a fireworks display (left), and many Jewish pilgrims travel to Jerusalem for the Sukkot festival (right).

thanksgiving. Often the general public is invited to these services. Older Jews remember that in their childhood Sukkot celebrations were street fairs and Sukkot was the happiest day of the year.

Hanukkah usually comes in December. Like other Jewish holidays, it has its foundation in history.

When Antiochus IV insisted that the Jews worship Zeus in the temple that they had dedicated to the "Holy Presence," the Hasmoneans, the father and five sons, became the leaders of an angry and successful revolt. Judas Maccabaeus, the third son, was the great military leader who conquered the despots and cleansed the temple. According to legend, there was only one vessel of oil for the dedication of the temple—just enough for one day—but the lamp burned for eight.

Now at Hanukkah one additional candle on an eight-branched menorah is lighted each day until all eight are burning.

In many Jewish homes Hanukkah is celebrated much as Christians celebrate Christmas, with feasts and gifts as well as with religious services.

The feast of Purim, in March, is based on events recounted in the biblical Book of Esther. According to the story, a Persian official named Haman sought to have Ahasuerus, the king, order the killing of all of the Jews in his kingdom. The beautiful Queen Esther, herself a Jew, had other ideas. Goaded by her cousin Mordecai, who had reared her, she went directly to the king. She told Ahasuerus about Haman's wicked proposal. Since Mordecai had once saved the king's life, the king punished Haman instead of killing all the Jews.

At Purim the Book of Esther is read from a scroll. This is the sacred part of the ceremony, but much goes on in the streets. Every house, every hotel, every street is filled with celebrating people. Everywhere there is laughter and merrymaking. Children carry gifts of special foods and wine to the homes of friends. Groups of costumed children enact the story. On every street there are little Esthers, little Mordecais, little Ahasueruses, even little Hamans.

During Purim there is much visiting and not even a stranger is turned away from a Jewish door.

The Passover is a festival of freedom. On the American Liberty Bell there is a statement from Moses: "Proclaim liberty throughout the land to all inhabitants thereof." The incredible Exodus of the Israelites to freedom is a reminder to everyone that man should not tolerate living in chains.

The celebration marks the greatest historical movement in Jewish history. According to the account in the Book of Exodus, one of the plagues that caused the Egyptian pharaoh to let the enslaved Israelites leave Egypt was that on an appointed night the firstborn of every living family died. Israelite families who marked their doors with the blood of a lamb were spared, as the angel of death passed over them. This is the limited meaning of the word Passover, but it has come to include the entire Exodus to freedom.

On the first night of the Passover and usually also on the second night, Jews in Israel and throughout the world partake of the festive meal called the seder. The Haggadah, the story of the Exodus, is read during the seder. Participants imagine themselves slaves, as their ancient forefathers were, and celebrate their freedom from those intolerable conditions.

After the recitation of the Haggadah by the family and guests, they all sing religious songs and play games that include even the smallest children. At the dinner table there is an empty chair and an extra glass for Elijah the prophet. Sometime during the seder the door is thrown open for him. When he enters he will bring news of the coming of the Messiah.

The Jews' hope is symbolized by the celebration of Passover. To many, the Passover marks the birth of the nation of Israel.

CHRISTIAN HOLIDAYS

Every day of the year the narrow streets of Old Jerusalem are crowded with Christian pilgrims, eager to see what Jesus saw, to walk where Jesus walked. There is so much eagerness on the part of Christians the world over that tourism has been one of the leading businesses for many years.

But Christmas is something special. Pilgrims look out over the meadows where the shepherds watched their sheep; they visit the shrines that have been built in sacred places since the time of Constantine. At Christmastime there are special services in the churches and at the Garden Tomb, even though no one knows the exact date, not even the time of year, when Christ was born.

An Armenian Orthodox Easter service in Jerusalem

When Christ came into Jerusalem for the last time, he was greeted with crowds waving palm branches. Now on Palm Sunday, pilgrims carrying palms start a procession at the Mount of Olives, go down to Gethsemane and across the Kidron Valley, entering Jerusalem by the Lion's Gate and ending in the courtyard of the Crusaders' Church of St. Anne. Palm Sunday is not a major holiday, but to people who have participated it is a high religious experience.

Certainly the greatest Christian celebration is at Easter. Although pilgrims climb the Via Dolorosa at all times of the year, at Easter the way is thronged with worshipers who feel increased fervor.

The Via Dolorosa begins at the probable site of the praetorium where Jesus was sentenced. There are fourteen stations where he might have stopped to rest. Each of these is marked in some way—by a church, a chapel, a shrine, a piece of ancient column.

Although no one knows whether or not this is the path that Jesus followed, countless thousands have walked the Via Dolorosa. The Via Dolorosa with its special stations of the cross was developed during the Ottoman period. The stations of the cross were mentioned in sixteenth-century pilgrims' letters, and the present Via Dolorosa was formalized in the middle of the nineteeth century.

MUSLIM HOLIDAYS

For Muslims there are many religious holidays. There is special commemoration of Muhammad's birth and of each of the special occasions in his life. There are celebrations for the births of other important Islamic leaders. These holidays are figured on the Islamic lunar calendar. This calendar marks its months by the stages of the moon, as other lunar calendars do, but its "year one" is actually A.D. 622 by the Gregorian calendar. This is the date of the *Hegira*, when Muhammad fled from Mecca. The Islamic sun calendar is figured from the seasons, as are all solar calendars. In order to keep pace with the rest of the world, Muslims also use the Gregorian calendar.

Ramadan is the most important celebration of all. It lasts a whole month. During the ninth month of the Islamic calendar, no Muslim eats between sunrise and sunset. This commemorates the period in Muhammad's life when he received most of the Koran. The Koran is the Muslim holy book which contains not only

Five times a day, Muslims are called to prayers by a muezzin (crier),
who speaks from the minaret (tower) of a mosque. The Ahmed Jezzar Mosque
in Acre (above) was built in 1781 on the site of a Crusader cathedral.

religious teachings, but all Islamic law. The celebration is in
gratitude for this most important gift.

Why the fast? Muhammad once fasted in the wilderness. In this
month all of his followers can share with him the feeling of
fasting.

Just as important as the fast is the reading of the Koran in every
mosque. Now it is read over modern loudspeakers so that the
voice of the mullah can be heard over all the Arab lands. It is
always read in Arabic.

At the end of a month's fasting, at sunset on the last day of the
month, there is a great feast. In even the poorest home there is
special food. Muslims believe in giving and sharing. Those who
have plenty give food to the poor on this occasion. Sometimes the
food is passed out after the last Ramadan service at the mosque,
just as the worshipers leave.

Chapter 8

CULTURE

The Jews have always been interested in culture and education. Even when they were scattered not only through Palestine but as far away as Russia, Iraq, and Yemen, they continued to study, to interpret the law, to produce literature. In the third century, Jewish scholars made Tiberias on the Sea of Galilee a center of learning. In the sixteenth century Palestine enjoyed a golden age of legal and mystical learning.

Wherever the European Jews formed communities throughout Europe, there were eager scholars among them, and literature and science as well as law prospered. In America, Jews have reached the highest point of creativity in science and medicine, in history, in the arts, and in literature.

IMMIGRANTS

When immigrants come to Israel, they are faced with a new language, different ways of doing things, a strange environment. To help them feel at home there are special six-month classes they can attend. They have come speaking English, or French, or Russian, or half a hundred other languages. Hebrew is the official language of Israel. It was once as dead as classical Greek or Latin, but now it is spoken in every home and government office, and on the street corner. In six months immigrants can learn the language. They also learn something about the customs, what is expected of them in a democracy, where the markets are, where their children will go to school, and what the educational opportunities are in their new areas. They are prepared for a new way of life, not thrust into one.

THE CHILDREN

Free elementary education is offered to children. They are required to go to school until they are fifteen. Most children, unless they are so poor that their families need financial assistance, go on to upper secondary school, although this isn't required. The students may prepare to enter a university or they may take technical or vocational courses and prepare to go directly into a trade or industry. Young apprentices, for example, are working in the aircraft industry. The secondary schools also offer arts and crafts, speech and drama, music, and sports.

UNIVERSITIES

In Israel there are twelve universities and technical institutes. Perhaps the most outstanding is Hebrew University, with two campuses, one on Mount Scopus and the other in West Jerusalem. The Hadassah Medical Center and Medical School was built in 1961 when Jordan denied the Jews the use of the hospital on Mount Scopus. It is one of the most modern facilities in the Middle East. The hospital has eight hundred beds, schools of

In addition to the original Hebrew University campus on Mount Scopus (top left), a western campus has been built. One of the buildings on the new campus is a modern synagogue (top right). These students (left) attend school at the modern high-school complex at Kibbutz Shefayim (right).

The library at Ben-Gurion University in Beersheba (left) is one of the futuristic buildings on this modern campus. At the Technion in Haifa, a chemist works in one of the laboratories (right).

medicine, nursing, dentistry, and pharmacology, a cancer research center, and an outpatient clinic that serves more than a thousand patients a day. Hebrew University offers undergraduate and graduate degrees. Other important universities are Tel Aviv University and the Technion in Haifa.

At Rehovot the Weizmann Institute of Science was established by friends of Chaim Weizmann, who was a great scientist and Israel's first president. Applied mathematics, biophysics, organic chemistry, physics, and a dozen other specialized sciences are taught at Weizmann Institute.

In Israel there is no shortage of great professors nor of students who are curious and competent.

*Imaginative exhibits at the Diaspora Museum in Tel Aviv (left) tell
the dramatic story of Jewish history throughout the world.
This Henry Moore sculpture (right) is part of the Billy Rose Sculpture
Garden display at the Israel Museum complex in Jerusalem.*

LIBRARIES AND MUSEUMS

In Israel almost six hundred magazines and newspapers are
published. With so much interest in reading, it is not surprising
that the country supports many public libraries. The National
Library is the largest, and its collections are of the greatest value.

Showing even more clearly the intellectual interests of the
people are the museums: the Israel Museum in Jerusalem, the Tel
Aviv Museum, Haifa's Museums of Modern Art and Ancient Art,
and many others. For students who want to know more of the
rich archaeological discoveries made in their land there is the
display of ancient art in Haifa Museum. Of special interest to
young people is the Biblical Zoo. All of the animals there are
mentioned in the Bible.

The Israel Philharmonic Orchestra, under the direction of Zubin Mehta, performs at the Frederic Mann Auditorium in Tel Aviv.

THEATER

Tel Aviv is the center of theater arts in Israel. The city has five publicly supported theaters and many independent playhouses. Most performances are in Hebrew, but English-speaking tourists can always find something in English.

MUSIC

Music is dear to the hearts of Israelis. The Israel Philharmonic Orchestra, under the direction of Zubin Mehta, is one of the world's greatest orchestras. The people appreciate it; 32,000 are subscribers. The Frederic Mann Auditorium in Tel Aviv is its home, but it plays some of its eighty yearly concerts in Jerusalem and Haifa. The musicians are highly professional and are noted for their independent views about the concert scores. Yet, in concert, when they are under Zubin Mehta's baton, their music is superb.

Three other orchestras are the Jerusalem, the Haifa, and the Galilee. In addition to these great orchestras there are many chamber groups, as well as a number of other small groups that play folk music or the classics. The United Kibbutz Orchestra and Choir sponsored by the kibbutz movement is of special interest to Israelis.

Many Israeli musicians have become world famous. Best known in America is Itzhak Perlman, who is, perhaps, the best-loved violinst in the world. He was born in Tel Aviv in 1945 and began his study at the Tel Aviv Academy of Music. When he was ten he gave his first solo recital. Later he studied at the Juilliard School of Music in New York.

He has played with every great orchestra and given recitals all over the world. His playing is superb. He has a beautiful expressive face on which the emotion he is feeling in his music is clearly drawn. American television audiences, people who might never have been able to go to a live concert, have heard him and loved him. Perlman is to the world a symbol of the devotion, skill, and pride that Israel puts into its music and its culture.

ART

Art is everywhere: in the displays of fine filigree work and embroidery in the bazaars of Jerusalem and Old Jaffa, and in the paintings and sculpture in the fine museums. There are several continuing art fairs, such as the one on the side of Mount Zion which was once a part of no-man's-land. This art center is surrounded by studios and shops. The winding streets of Jaffa are crowded with studios and shops and an art colony has grown up around it. Art appreciation is taught in the public schools.

In Acre, an artist has painted a mural on a wall in the old city.

In addition to paintings and sculpture, some of the finest stained-glass windows that have been made since the Gothic period crown the synagogue at the Hadassah Hospital. Made by Jewish artist Marc Chagall, the twelve windows depict the twelve tribes of Israel.

FOLK CUSTOMS

With all of this rich cultural life the old times are not forgotten. The people tell the folktales, dance the folk dances, sing the folk songs, and on many occasions dress in native dress. Sometimes spring planting and fall harvesting are celebrated with impromptu parades and festivals.

In spite of the time, money, and energy that the Israelis have had to spend in defending their country, they have never lost the love of the beautiful. From the kindergarten child to the patron of the arts in Tel Aviv or Jerusalem or Haifa, the people delight in beauty.

Chapter 9

SPECIAL PEOPLE AND PLACES

Special people? Our thoughts go first to the great scientists whose work has done so much to prevent and treat disease. These are Jewish scientists, but are they Israeli? What great Israeli men and women have had a part in building and preserving the country?

THEODOR HERZL

Theodor Herzl (1860-1904) was the father of modern political Zionism. He didn't dream of a Jewish state when he was a child in Budapest, Hungary, or as a law student, or as a staff writer for *Neue Freie Presse* in Vienna, Austria. It was an appointment as a newspaper foreign correspondent in Paris that changed his life and gave him a special dream.

In 1894 a young French army officer, Alfred Dreyfus, was accused of passing written information about the French army to the Germans. Although there was little evidence, and Dreyfus himself declared that he was innocent, the military court convicted him of high treason and banished him to Devil's Island, an isolated prison colony off the coast of French Guiana.

Theodor Herzl, the father of modern Zionism, dreamed of making Palestine a Jewish homeland.

Dreyfus was a Jew, and many thought that this was the real reason for his trial, his conviction, and his banishment.

Herzl read the newspapers and found them violently anti-Semitic (anti-Jewish). He was horrified to feel this spirit in many of the French people as well as in the press. He came to the conclusion that anti-Semitic passion wasn't a passing thing. He felt it had been ingrained over the centuries and that it could never be eradicated. The only way that Jews could be happy and productive, he thought, was to live in a state of their own.

He had returned to Vienna and was the literary editor of *Neue Freie Presse* before new trials freed Alfred Dreyfus, but the cause of the Jews had grown beyond the Dreyfus case. In 1896 Herzl published *The Jewish State*. This state, as he dreamed it, would be progressive and modern, using all the advanced ideas that were being developed in Europe and America.

Where would that state be? Herzl probably got the idea that it should be in Palestine from the "Love of Zion" group. These people believed that Palestine was the destined place for Jews to make a homeland, and Herzl agreed. He tried to get statesmen from powerful countries to help him obtain "a land without people" for "a people without land."

To gain support for making Palestine a homeland for the Jews, he became head of the worldwide Zionist movement. The organization had a newspaper, *The World,* and a financial support system, the Jewish Colonial Trust. The first Zionist Congress was assembled by Herzl in Switzerland in 1897. He had a winning personality that made the Jewish people love and trust him and become enthusiastic about his cause.

There were some doubters, among them rabbis who said that the Jews should stay where they were, where they had been for centuries. Wherever they were they could be excellent citizens. They thought that the Zionist dream of a Jewish homeland was absurd and unworkable.

Herzl died in 1904, his dream unrealized. But how much this father of Zionism had done in a lifetime! Now Israelis honor him as a founding father of modern Israel. Countless streets and other sites are named after him, and his picture hangs in the Knesset.

CHAIM WEIZMANN

Chaim Weizmann (1874-1952) was born in Russian Poland. Unlike Theodor Herzl, he grew up in a traditional Jewish home. He was a brilliant student, and when he was ready for advanced education he studied biochemistry in Germany and Switzerland. At Geneva he became a lecturer, and in 1904 at Manchester,

Chaim Weizmann served as president of Israel until his death in 1952.

England, a scholar. He was a Zionist, believing actively in a national home for the Jews in Palestine, and became the Zionist leader in England. He had a charismatic personality, he spoke several languages, and his work on acetone was extremely valuable to the British war effort from 1916 to 1918.

The British statesmen liked and admired him, and it was largely because of his influence that Britain declared in the Balfour Declaration that it favored the establishment of a Jewish national home in Palestine.

In 1920 Weizmann became president of the World Zionist Organization, and was the principal spokesman for the Jew before British and international commissions.

He retired to Rehovot from 1946 to 1948 to work at the Institute of Science, now known as the Weizmann Institute. Then in 1948 the state of Israel came into being. Weizmann was the first president of the provisional state. In 1949 he became president of Israel and served until his death in 1952.

David Ben-Gurion, one of the earliest Eastern European settlers in Palestine, was a farmer, politician, statesman, warrior, and writer.

DAVID BEN-GURION

The short, stocky, dynamic David Ben-Gurion (1886-1973) was the father of his country. He was political leader, statesman, prime minister, and the real architect of the state of Israel. The people adored him for his charismatic personality and for his fighting spirit.

He was born in 1886 in Plonsk, Poland, to parents who had already felt the stirring of the desire to return to Zion. His father was a leader in the "Love of Zion" movement. David didn't remember when he wasn't fascinated by the idea of oppressed Jews escaping the hardships of Jewish life in Europe by immigrating to Palestine and building farms for themselves.

In 1906 he carried out his dream. He arrived in Palestine. He didn't have any money, but then he hadn't expected a life of ease. He went to work on the coastal plains and near the Sea of Galilee as a farmer. He had been born David Gruen, but in Palestine—there was no Israel then—he changed it to Ben-Gurion.

In 1907, at a convention of the Young Workers party, Ben-Gurion insisted on including in its platform this statement: "The Party aspires to the political independence of the Jewish people in this land."

Turkey controlled Palestine at this time and when World War I started, the officials arrested Ben-Gurion and expelled him from the Ottoman Empire. Since he was exiled rather than imprisoned he traveled to New York, where he married Pauline Munweis.

In 1917 he was overjoyed when Britain passed the Balfour Declaration. He hurried back to enlist in the British army's Jewish legion. Now he would have a chance to fight for the liberation of Palestine. When he arrived, the Turks were already defeated. He didn't know then how many times he would have the opportunity to fight or who one of his greatest enemies would be.

Ben-Gurion called for more and more people to immigrate to Palestine so that there would be a foundation for a Jewish state. In 1920 he helped to organize the Histadrut, which was to become the nucleus of the new state, and was elected its first secretary-general.

By then Ben-Gurion had realized that he was not a farmer. When the political party Mapai was formed, he was its head. In 1935 he was elected head of the Zionist Executive and of the Jewish Agency.

In 1948 he became both prime minister and defense minister of the new state of Israel. Several underground armies had fought the British. He, with his personal charisma, fused them into one fighting force. No one was more pleased than Ben-Gurion to see the history of the Jewish state go on after a two-thousand-year interruption.

What were his policies? He aimed to absorb more immigration, assimilate the newcomers, create a unified and excellent public school system, and settle the desert land. "What matters is not what the gentiles will say, but what the Jews will do" were his words, and his foreign policy was firm: "Don't tread on us."

Ben-Gurion—farmer, politician, statesman, warrior—became a writer in 1963 when he moved to a kibbutz in the Negev and put his dreams and aspirations for Israel into writing. He died in 1973.

GOLDA MEIR

Golda Meir (1898-1978) was born Goldie Mabovitch in Kiev, Russia. Her first memory was of watching her father and other men boarding up their houses, fearing a Cossack attack. When that job was finished the fathers gave their children sticks to defend themselves. Golda thought, "What use is this stick when I am so small?" The Cossacks didn't come that year but they came the next, their horses' hooves pounding over the cobbled streets. Forty-five men, women, and children were killed and more than a thousand homes and shops were looted and destroyed. The Jews couldn't retaliate. Instead they went to their synagogue and prayed and fasted. Although Golda was only five, she insisted on fasting all day. That was her first strike for freedom.

Her father had had enough of persecutions. In 1903 he emigrated to America and in 1906 the rest of the family joined him in Milwaukee, Wisconsin.

Golda was excited about going to school, and she learned English very rapidly. The elementary school didn't provide free books, and while Golda was still a grade-school student she organized the American Young Sister Society to get free textbooks for poor children to give them an equal chance. They rented a hall

Golda Meir, who arrived in Palestine in 1921, was prime minister of Israel from 1969 to 1974.

and gave a program. The main speech was given by Golda. Her speech was so fiery and the two Yiddish poems she recited so appealing to the largely Jewish audience, that it made the front page of the papers. Golda was already an organizer and an orator.

When Golda was older, she taught in the public schools of Milwaukee. But she wasn't happy. She felt strongly that her place was in Palestine. In 1915 she joined the Zionist Labor Organization. In 1921 with her husband, Morris Myerson, she emigrated to Palestine. In Palestine she changed her name to its Hebrew form, Meir, which means "to burn brightly."

After two years, Golda rose in position and responsibility. She was high in the women's council of the Histadrut and was named to the Histadrut executive committee in 1934. In 1946 she became president of the political bureau of the Jewish Agency.

In 1948 she became Israel's minister to Moscow and in 1969 was chosen prime minister. Golda spent the next four years working for peace in the Middle East. When the October 1973 Arab-Israeli war found Israel largely unprepared, the nation lost confidence in Meir. She eventually resigned in 1974.

And what of her life as Mrs. Myerson? The distance grew between the gentle, loving Morris, who wanted nothing but a pleasant home and children, and the vibrant, vigorous Golda, until a separation was inevitable. She had two children, a son and a daughter, and before her death in 1978, grandchildren.

Because the Western Wall functions as an Orthodox synagogue, men and women worshipers are segregated (left). Before morning prayers at the wall, a rabbi helps a young Jewish man don his phylacteries, small leather boxes containing scriptures that are bound to the forehead and left arm (right).

THE WESTERN WALL

On the western edge of Jerusalem's Temple Square on Mount Moriah stands the Western Wall, also known as the Wailing Wall. One of the Jews' most venerated sites, the wall itself is not so sacred as what lies beyond it. Within the Temple Square once stood the temple with its Holy of Holies, a chamber that only the high priest could enter. As the exact location of the Holy of Holies is unknown, devout Jews never enter the square for fear of walking on the holy ground.

The area around the wall now functions as a synagogue, where Sabbath and holy day services are held and where worshipers can be seen in prayer twenty-four hours a day.

The Garden of Gethsemane, where Jesus prayed before his death

THE MOUNT OF OLIVES

Through the Lion's Gate in the eastern wall of Old Jerusalem lies the Kidron Valley. Across this valley lies the Mount of Olives. To Christians this is a most sacred place. Near the foot of the mount is Gethsemane, the garden where Jesus prayed before his death while his disciples slept. The Basilica of the Agony was built here in the fourth century, and its place has been taken by a modern church built in the 1920s. Since people all over the world contributed toward its building and its magnificent frescoes, it is called the Church of the Nations.

Behind Gethsemane rises the mount. On its summit is the Church of the Ascension, and at its foot the Tomb of Mary.

It isn't the magnificent buildings, old or new, on these sacred sites that move pilgrims to tears. To feel the quiet of the olive grove is to feel a deeper spirit. Perhaps Jesus sought peace under one of these same trees. Perhaps these trees, that may have seen the actual happenings, are the real links to the past.

This replica of the ghetto memorial at Dachau by Nandor Glid stands on the grounds of Yad Vashem, a shrine that memorializes the six million victims of the Nazi Holocaust.

YAD VASHEM MEMORIAL

What a leap from the suffering of two thousand years ago to the suffering in our own century! Yad Vashem, in Jerusalem, is a shrine to memorialize the victims of the Holocaust. Here there is a sacred flame that is different from any other. It burns over the ashes of people who died because they were Jews. The ashes were brought from the concentration camps.

Next to the shrine are a museum, a library, and a reading room where archives of the Holocaust are kept. A beautiful black basalt memorial is at the entrance. The Jews living in the ghettos of Europe were doomed to die, yet they had the courage and heroic spirit to resist. The monument commemorates not only the victims, but their indomitable spirit.

THE CHAGALL WINDOWS

The twelve stained-glass windows that crown the synagogue of the Hadassah Medical Center are most unusual.

Marc Chagall, the artist who created the windows, was not born in Israel. He was born and reared in a small Jewish town in

Marc Chagall's stained-glass windows in the Hadassah Medical Center synagogue depict the twelve tribes of Israel. These two show the tribes of Levi (left) and Zebulun (right).

Russia. He was educated to share the Jewish dreams. The Bible was his first book, and throughout his life, his favorite. The miracles were real to him, and because he always thought in pictures he saw the stories long before he produced his art.

In 1931 he visited the Holy Land and began to produce his biblical art.

He was seventy-two when Hadassah commissioned him to make the stained-glass windows. He accepted with delight. Twelve windows? That would give a window to each of the sons of Jacob and the tribes they founded. But in Jewish religious art, human forms cannot be used. How could he commemorate the twelve sons of Jacob (Israel) and tell something of their personalities and achievements? He would do it with symbols, with fish and birds and animals, with spheres and boats and arrows and trees. He would do it with color from the softest pastels to the most brilliant red, yellow, purple, green, and blue.

He took the designs for the windows through many drafts, using a variety of materials. With the help of two young artists, Carles and Brigitte Simon-Marc, who were famous for their stained glass, the windows were finished according to his visions and set in place.

There is nothing like them in the world. Viewers can look at them and enjoy the jewel-like color. Bible students can repeat the blessings Jacob gave to his sons, and read the meanings in the fluttering bird wings or the crying fish.

To see the Chagall windows is a never-to-be-forgotten experience.

MASADA

Just west of Israel's Dead Sea a great rock, 1,300 feet (396 meters) high, rises from the desert floor. Up the west side of the sheer cliff is a footpath, easy for most people to climb. On the east face of the rock is a "snake path," with rest and water stops, that is steep and difficult. But for those who are old or tired there is a cable car running partway to the summit. Why all this interest in reaching the top of the rock? It isn't to absorb the beauty of the blue waters of the lowest sea in the world or to look east to the pink hills of Moab. It isn't to look with wonder at the remains of Herod's three-tiered palaces with their amazing frescoes. Rather, it is to remember the history of Masada and to absorb the spirit of those who died there.

A group of Jews living at Masada refused to surrender to the Romans after the fall of Jerusalem in A.D. 70. Two years later, the Romans decided to break this last holdout, and surrounded the rock to attack.

The three-tiered palace at Masada, built by King Herod on the site of an earlier Jewish fortress, was captured by a group of Jewish rebels in A.D. 66. Rather than surrender to Roman troops who were about to recapture the fortress in A.D. 73, the Jews burned their camp and killed themselves. Masada has become a symbol of liberty to Israeli Jews, who swear that "Masada shall not fall again."

The Jews' leader, Eleazar Ben Yair, called his people together. There were only two options: surrender and become slaves or die. They discussed these two terrible options and decided that death would be better than slavery. And so that night the entire group— 960 men, women, and children—chose suicide. Perhaps some were chosen as executioners. The pottery shards found in the excavation of Masada may have been lots drawn for this grisly task. At least one of them bears the name of Eleazar Ben Yair.

Next day when the Romans entered they found absolute silence. They found 960 dead. They not only were cheated of their victory, they were amazed. Who would have the courage to accept death to avoid losing liberty? When the Jews of Israel cry, "Masada shall not fall again," it is their way of saying what Patrick Henry said at the time of the American Revolution, "Give me liberty or give me death."

About seven thousand Israelis live on the Golan Heights, a disputed territory annexed by Israel in 1981.

Someday you may visit Israel. You may go as a tourist who wishes to see the ancient ruins, shop in the bazaars and designer shops, bathe in the waters of the Mediterranean, the Sea of Galilee, or the Red Sea, hear the famous orchestra, and see the vitality of the folk dancing.

You may be a Christian who has longed to walk where Jesus walked. You may travel from the Sea of Galilee to Jerusalem. You may see all of the sacred shrines. You may choose Christmas for its high mass at the nativity site. You may prefer Easter and stumble up the Via Dolorosa, stopping at the stations of the cross, even help to carry the great wooden cross like the one that Jesus carried on his shoulder.

Or you may be a Jew, really coming home. You will hear the Hebrew that you learned for your bar or bat mitzvah spoken as an everyday language. You will feel the energy and bustle once felt in the western frontier towns of the United States as you visit the kibbutzim as well as the cities. And last, you will climb to the top of Masada. Tears will fill your eyes as you repeat to yourself, "Masada shall not fall again." You will have heard the voice of Israel.

MAP KEY

(Cities in the West Bank, Gaza Strip, and Golan Heights are included here as well.)

'Abasān (Gaza Strip)	C6	Hanita	A7	Pardes Hanna	B6
Acre ('Akko)	B7	Halhūl (West Bank)	C7	Petah Tiqwa	B6
'Afula	B7	Har Ramon (mountain)	D6	Qabātiyah (West Bank)	B7
Al Fandaqūmīyah (West Bank)	B7	Hazor	A,B7	Qalqīlyah (West Bank)	B6
Al Khushnīyah (Golan Heights)	B7	Hebron (Al Khalīl,		Qezi'ot	D6
An Nazlah (Gaza Strip)	C6	West Bank)	C7	Qiryat Gat	C6
'Aqrabah (West Bank)	B7	Herzliyya	B6	Qiryat 'Anavim	C7
'Arrābah (West Bank)	B7	Holon	B6	Qiryat Mal'akhi	C6
Ashdod	C6	Jabālyah (Gaza Strip)	C6	Qiryat Shemona	A7
Ashqelon	C6	Janīn (West Bank)	B7	Qiryat Yam	B7
As Samū' (West Bank)	C7	Jericho (Arīha, West Bank)	C7	Qishon (river)	B7
'Atlit	B6	Jerusalem (Yerushalayim)	C7	Rafah (Gaza Strip)	C6
Aṭ Ṭayyibah (West Bank)	C7	Jordan (river)	B,C7	Rām Allāh (West Bank)	C7
'Awartā (West Bank)	B7	Judean Hills	C6,7	Rama	B7
Az Ẓāhiriyah (West Bank)	C6	Karkur	B6	Ramat Gan	B6
Banī Na'īm (West Bank)	C7	Kefar Ata	B7	Ramla	C6
Bani Suheila (Gaza Strip)	C6	Kefar Blum	A7	Rehovot	C6
Bāniyās (Golan Heights)	A7	Kefar Sava	B6	Revivim	C6
Bāqa el Gharbiyya	B7	Khān Yūnus (Gaza Strip)	C6	Rishon le Ziyyon	C6
Bay of Haifa (Mifraz Hefa)	B6,7	Khisfīn (Golan Heights)	B7	Rosh Ha'Ayin	B6
Bayt Jālā (West Bank)	C7	Kuneitra (Al Qunayṭirah,		Rosh Haniqra	A7
Beersheba (Be'er Sheva')	C6	Golan Heights)	A7	Rosh Pinna	B7
Bene Berit	B7	Laṭrūn (West Bank)	C6	Safad (Zefat)	B7
Bet Guvrin	C6	Lod (Lydda)	C6	Salfīt (West Bank)	B7
Bet She'an	B7	Ma'alot-Tarshiḥa	A,B7	Scrolls Caves (West Bank)	C7
Bet Shemesh	C6	Mas'adah (Golan Heights)	A7	Sea of Galilee (Yam Kinneret)	B7
Bethlehem (Bayt Laḥm, West		Mash'abbe Sade	C,D6	Sederot	C6
Bank)	C7	Mediterranean Sea	A,B,C 6,7	Sedom	C7
Binyamina	B6	Metulla	A7	Sedot Yam	B6
Buṭayḥah (Golan Heights)	B7	Migdal	B7	Shefar'am	B7
Dāliyat el Karmel	B7	Mizpe Ramon	D6	Si'īr (West Bank)	C7
Dayr al Balaḥ (Gaza Strip)	C6	Mt. Carmel (Har Hakarmel)	B7	Tammūn (West Bank)	B7
Dead Sea	C7	Mt. Heron (Hare Meron)	A7	Tel Aviv-Yafo	B6
Dimona	C6,7	Mt. Tabor (Har Tavor)	B7	Tel Mond	B6
Dura (West Bank)	C7	Nābulus (West Bank)	B7	Tiberias (Teverya)	B7
Elat (Elath; Eilat)	E6	Nahal Hemar	C7	Tirat Karmel	B6
'En Gedi	C7	Nahal Nizzana	D6	Tirat Zevi	B7
'En Harod	B7	Nahal Paran	D6	Tūbas (West Bank)	B7
Eṭ Ṭaiyiba (West Bank)	B7	Nahal Ramon	C6	Tulkarm (West Bank)	B7
Eṭ Ṭira	B6	Nahal Zin	D6,7	Turmus 'Ayyā (West Bank)	B7
Fiq (Golan Heights)	B7	Nahariyya	A,B7	Umm el Fahm (West Bank)	B7
Galilee (region)	B7	Na'rān (Golan Heights)	A7	Ya'bad	B7
Gaza (Ghazzah, Gaza Strip)	C6	Nazareth (Nazerat)	B7	Yad Mordekhay	C6
Gedera	C6	Negev Desert (Hānegev)	D6,7	Yagon (river)	B6
Gesher HaZiw	A7	Nes Ziyyona	C6	Yarqon (river)	B6
Gulf of Aqaba	E6	Nesher	B7	Yaṭṭah (West Bank)	C7
Ha'Arava (depression)	D7	Netanya	B6	Yavne	C6
Hadera	B6	Ofaqim	C6	Yotvata	E7
Haifa (Hefa)	B6	Or-'Aquiva	B6	Zikhron Ya'aqov	B6

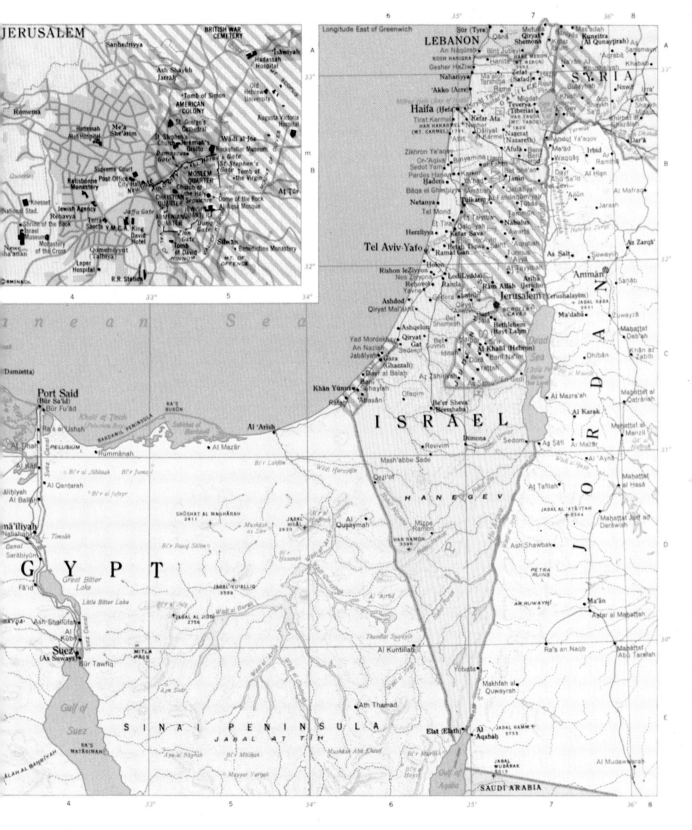

MINI-FACTS AT A GLANCE

GENERAL INFORMATION

Official Name: State of Israel *(Medinat Yisrael)*

Capital: Jerusalem

Official Languages: Hebrew and Arabic

Government: Israel is a democratic republic with a parliamentary system of government. The Knesset, or assembly, is a 120-member, single-chamber legislature that is elected every four years. The president, who is head of state, is elected by the Knesset for a five-year term. The prime minister, appointed by the president, forms and heads the cabinet, which also must have the Knesset's vote of confidence. Voting age is eighteen.

Courts: The ten-member Supreme Court is the highest court. Judges are appointed by the president for life. Religious courts handle some personal matters.

Coat of Arms: Israel's coat of arms shows the menorah, the ancient holy candleholder. The menorah is surrounded by two olive branches linked at the bottom by the inscription "Israel," in Hebrew.

Flag: Soon after its conception, the Zionist movement adopted a flag of its own. It consisted of a white field with two horizontal blue stripes and the Magen David (Shield of David) in its center. The Zionist flag became the official banner when the state of Israel was established. The choice of colors was inspired by the blue and white of the tallith (prayer shawl).

National Song: *"Hatikva"* ("The Hope")

Religion: Jews make up about 90 percent of the people of Israel. The largest religious minority group is the Muslims, who total about 80 percent of all Israeli Arabs. Other religious groups include Christians, Druzes, and Baha'is.

Armed Forces: Israel requires Jewish men and most unmarried Jewish women to serve in the armed forces after reaching the age of eighteen. Men are drafted for three years, and women for two years. The nation does not draft its Arab citizens (although they may volunteer), but other non-Jews are drafted. The regular Israeli army has about 150,000 men and women and some 370,000 reservists.

Sculpture of a menorah in Jerusalem (left), and two young boys at the Western Wall (right)

Population: 4,164,000 (1986 estimate). Distribution is about 91 percent urban and 9 percent rural. Density is 518 persons per sq. mi. (200 per km²).

Cities: The largest cities (1982 official estimate) are:

Jerusalem	424,400
Tel Aviv-Jaffa	325,700
Haifa	266,100
Holon	134,600
Bat Yam	134,500
Petah Tiqwa	124,000

Money: Money in Israel is based on the shekel. The shekel was introduced in 1980 to replace the Israeli pound at a rate of 1 shekel for every 10 pounds. The shekel consists of 100 agorot. The denominations of the new shekel are 1, 5, 10, 50, and 100. On May 9, 1986, the U.S. dollar bought 1.3 shekels.

A tributary of the Jordan River in Banias, Golan Heights

GEOGRAPHY

Highest Point: Mount Meron, 3,963 ft. (1,208 m)

Lowest Point: The Dead Sea, 1,310 ft. (399 m) below sea level

Area: 8,019 sq. mi. (20,770 km²)

Greatest Distances: North to south—256 mi. (412 km)
East to west—81 mi. (131 km)

Coastline: 134 mi. (230 km)

Land Regions: There are four main land regions in Israel: (1) the Mediterranean coastal plains, (2) the Judeo-Galilean highlands, (3) the Great Rift Valley, and (4) the Negev Desert.

Rivers: The River Jordan is the longest of Israel's rivers. Other rivers are the Qishon and the Yarqon, both found in the coastal plains region. The remaining streams, usually seasonal, flow through streambeds called wadis.

Wildflowers blooming near the Sea of Galilee

Climate: Israel has hot, dry summers and mild or cool winters. Temperature depends on elevation and distance from the sea. The hottest month, August, has an average temperature of 80° F. (28° C). The average temperature in January, the coolest month, is about 52° F. (11° C). In the south, rainfall is light, amounting to only about 1 in. (3 cm) per year. Approximately 40 in. (100 cm) of rain falls in the north each year.

Borders: North, Lebanon; east, Syria and Jordan; south, Egypt; west, Mediterranean Sea.

NATURE

Birds: There are over four hundred species of birds in Israel, including the partridge, tropical cuckoo, bustard, sand grouse, and desert lark.

Animals: Over two hundred species of mammals and reptiles live in Israel. Some mammals include wildcats, wild boars, gazelles, ibex, coneys, hyenas, and tiger weasels. Reptiles include the agama and gecko lizards and the carpet viper.

ECONOMY AND INDUSTRY

Minerals: Israel has limited mineral resources. They include potash, bromine, magnesium, copper ore, phosphates, gypsum, and marble. Deposits of oil and natural gas are also found, but supply less than 10 percent of the nation's fuel.

Electricity: Electricity is principally generated from thermal stations. A salt pool in the Dead Sea area is a solar energy source for electricity.

Manufacturing: Industrial growth has been especially rapid in electronics, weapons, transportation, machinery, and metals. One of the largest industrial enterprises is Israel Aircraft Industries. The diamond cutting and polishing industry ranks among the largest in the world.

Agriculture: Farmers, though few in number, are vital to Israel's economy, producing about three fourths of the country's food. The main farm products include oranges (Israel's chief product), other citrus fruits, eggs, milk, and poultry. Other important products are cotton, sugar beets, grain, and vegetables.

Irrigation: Water from the Jordan and Yarqon rivers and from the Sea of Galilee is pumped through the National Water Carrier. This is a system of canals, pipelines, and tunnels that is 88.5 mi. (142 km) long. A network of regional systems connects with the carrier and extends to the southern Negev.

EVERYDAY LIFE

Communication: Israel has about twenty-five daily newspapers, circulating more than 500,000 copies a day. The government operates the radio and television stations and the telegraph, postal, and telephone services. Hebrew is the language of most newspapers and radio broadcasts, but other languages used are Yiddish, French, German, and Russian. Television, which was introduced in 1966, consists of Hebrew and Arabic programs.

Transportation: Road transportation is more important than rail. Israel has about 2,400 mi. (3,860 km) of paved roads. A government-owned railroad connects all major cities and towns. The government operates El Al Israel Airlines, which flies to many countries from Ben-Gurion international airport. Airports at Jerusalem, Tel Aviv, Eilat, Rosh Pinna, and Haifa serve domestic air traffic. Three modern deep-water ports in Haifa, Ashod, and Eilat are maintained and developed by the Israel Ports Authority.

Education: Education is free and obligatory for children between the ages of five and thirteen. The high schools charge small tuitions. Public elementary schools include both religious and secular institutions for Jews. Jewish classes are in Hebrew; Arabic is used in Israel's Arab schools. Israel has several universities and colleges. The largest are Tel Aviv University and Hebrew University of Jerusalem. The Israel Institute of Technology, called Technion, is located in Haifa.

Holidays: Most holidays in Israel are fixed according to the lunar calendar. Here they are divided into seasons:

Spring:
    Passover (Pesach) — celebrating the exodus from Egypt
    Purim — commemorating the deliverance from Haman
    Independence Day — celebrating Israel's becoming a nation

Summer:
Shavuot—celebrates the giving of the Ten Commandments
Autumn:
Rosh Hashanah—Jewish New Year
Yom Kippur—Day of Atonement
Sukkot—Feast of Tabernacles, commemorating the Israelites' wandering in
the desert
Simhat Torah—Day of Rejoicing of the Law
Winter:
Hanukkah—Feast of Lights, commemorating the victory of the Maccabees

People in Israel celebrate holy days according to several calendars: Jews follow
the Hebrew, Muslims observe Islamic, and Christians follow either the Julian or the
Gregorian.

Health and Welfare: Israel's health-care standards have reduced its infant
mortality rate to among the world's lowest. The ratio of Israel's doctors to its
population (1 for every 415 persons) is among the world's highest. A National
Insurance Institute provides a broad range of benefits to all citizens.

Housing: Under a public housing program begun in the 1950s, an average of
thirty thousand new units have been built every year for young couples and new
immigrants. Some farms are privately owned, but most Israeli farmers belong to a
collective or cooperative community. Kibbutzim are collective groups, voluntarily
practicing joint production and consumption. Their farmers share all the property
and combine their labor. Moshavim are cooperatives practicing joint sales and
purchases and making common use of machinery. Both the kibbutzim and
moshavim perform pioneer work in underdeveloped areas and security functions
in border areas.

Food: Because Israel has immigrants from more than fifty countries, it offers a
diverse cuisine. The traditional dishes of different communities are adapted to local
products, climates, and tastes. The dishes traditionally associated with Sabbath and
Jewish festivals still occupy an important place. Because of the abundance of fresh
fruits and vegetables, salads are served often. Israel offers an almost endless variety
of breads, including pita, pumpernickel, rye, and halot. Other common foods
include felafel, sold by street vendors, and humus; both are made from ground
chick-peas. Meat eaten on a skewer is called kabob or shashlik. Dairy products such
as yogurt, cheeses, and sour cream are also important.

Sports: Basketball runs a close second to soccer as the nation's most popular
sport. The long summertime weather also makes water sports, tennis, handball,
volleyball, and yachting very popular. In the year following each Olympics, Israel
hosts the World Maccabiah games, an event that draws Jewish athletes from all
over the world. Marching is popular as a noncompetitive sport, the main event
being an annual four-day march to Jerusalem. A swim across Lake Kinneret also
takes place every year.

Culture: Because immigrants to Israel come from so many different countries, the creative arts are very diverse, but Western art forms predominate. The national theater, which was formed in Russia, has a worldwide reputation. Israel's national museum was opened in Jerusalem in 1965. There are numerous museums in Tel Aviv-Jaffa, Haifa, and other large towns and settlements.

IMPORTANT DATES

B.C.

c. 7500—Towns are settled in Middle East

c. 1250—Moses called to lead Israelites out of Egypt

c. 1250-1200—Joshua leads Israelites to Canaan

1006-965—David, as king, expands kingdom of Israel

965-928—King Solomon rules, builds the First Temple in Jerusalem

928—Kingdom splits into Judah and Israel

721—Northern Kingdom conquered by Sargon II of Assyria

587—Babylonians destroy Judah and the Temple; Jews exiled to Babylon

538—Cyrus the Great conquers Babylon, frees captive Jews

520-515—Solomon's temple rebuilt (known as Second Temple)

445—New city walls of Jerusalem completed

312-198—Ptolemies of Egypt rule Judea

198-167—Greek Seleucids are in power; temple is badly damaged

166-37—Period of Hasmonean rule

63—The Roman General Pompey conquers Jerusalem; Roman occupation begins

37—Herod the Great comes to power

20—Herod starts rebuilding the temple

A.D.

26 — Pontius Pilate becomes procurator of Judea

66-70 — Jewish uprisings against the Romans

70 — Titus sacks Jerusalem and destroys the temple; dispersal of Jews

132-135 — Bar Kokhba's war of freedom; Jerusalem again becomes capital

135 — Jerusalem destroyed by Romans, who then build on its ruins a new city called Aelia Capitolina; Jews banned from city

324 — Constantine the Great becomes Roman Emperor, declares Christianity the official religion; builds the Church of the Holy Sepulcher

614 — Persian conquest of Palestine

638 — Jerusalem conquered by Arabs (Muslim conquest)

c. 691 — Dome of the Rock completed

1099 — Jerusalem captured by the Crusaders; Jews and Muslims banned

1187 — Saladin captures Jerusalem from Crusaders, returns it to Muslim rule

1244 — Jerusalem conquered by Khwarizans

1516 — Palestine captured by Turks

1517-1917 — Ottoman Turks rule Palestine

1520-1566 — Sultan Suleiman rebuilds walls of Jerusalem

1860 — First Jewish settlement outside Jerusalem city walls

1878 — First Jewish agricultural settlement founded at Petah Tiqwa

1882-1903 — First *aliyah* (large scale Jewish "ascent," or immigration, to Palestine)

1904 — Beginning of second *aliyah*, bringing new idealism of "conquest of labor"

1917 — British conquest; General Allenby enters Jerusalem; Balfour Declaration issued

1919-1923 — Third *aliyah*

1922 — Churchill issues White Paper, British mandate commences

1929-1939 — Fifth *aliyah* (German Jews)

1936 — Arab uprising against British over Jewish immigration

1939 — Macdonald White Paper limits Jewish immigration and purchase of land

1939-1945 — Truce in struggle against British government for period of World War II

1946 — Flow of illegal immigrants diverted by British to Cyprus

1947 — U.N. resolution to divide Palestine into Jewish and Arab states is rejected by Arabs; Dead Sea Scrolls discovered

1948 — Proclamation of State of Israel; Arab armies attack on all sides; massive Jewish immigration

1949 — Cease-fire agreements signed by Israel with Jordan, Syria, Egypt, Lebanon, with U.N. help; first Knesset elections

1956 — Suez War; Israel attacks Egypt and occupies Gaza Strip and Sinai Peninsula

1957 — Israel evacuates Sinai, U.N. emergency forces sent to border

1967 — Egypt insists on removal of U.N. force; Six-Day War; Jerusalem reunited

1973 — Yom Kippur War; Egypt and Syria attack Israel

1976 — Israeli air force frees hostages kidnapped by Arab terrorists held in Entebbe, Uganda

1977 — Egyptian President Sadat and Israeli Prime Minister Begin meet in Jerusalem

1978 — Camp David Accords result from meeting of Sadat, Begin, and U.S. President Carter; Israel invades southern Lebanon and withdraws in favor of U.N. force

1979 — Egypt-Israel peace treaty signed

1981 — Israel destroys Iraqi atomic reactor

1982 — Israelis bomb PLO strongholds in Lebanon and encircle West Beirut; Egypt and Israel establish diplomatic relations

1983—Menachem Begin resigns as prime minister; Yitzhak Shamir succeeds him; defense minister resigns after being cited for neglect of duty during the massacre of Palestinian refugees in camps outside West Beirut.

1984—Parliamentary elections result in unity government; Labor party leader Shimon Peres takes office as prime minister for twenty-five months, to be followed by Shamir's twenty-five month term.

1987—A number of surprising political revelations, including Israel's role in U.S.-Iran-Contra scandal threaten stability of unity government

IMPORTANT PEOPLE

Shmuel Yosef Agnon (1888-1970), novelist and short story writer, shared the 1966 Nobel Prize in literature with Nelly Sachs "for his profoundly characteristic narrative art with motifs from the life of the Jewish people;" was born in eastern Galicia, now a part of Russia

Menachem Begin (b. 1913), prime minister of Israel from 1977 to 1983; born in Brest-Litovsk (now Brest), Russia

David Ben-Gurion (1886-1973), prime minister after independence in 1948; born David Gruen in Plonsk, Russia (now Poland); settled in Palestine in 1906

Itzhak Ben-Zvi (1884-1963), second president of the state of Israel; born in Poltava, Ukraine, Russia

Martin Buber (1878-1965), one of the greatest Jewish philosophers of modern times; a founder of Zionism, he was born in Vienna and settled in Jerusalem permanently in 1938

Moshe Dayan (1915-1981), military hero and political leader; born in Degania, Palestine; became Israel's foreign minister in 1977 and resigned in 1979

Yaël Dayan (b. 1939), daughter of Moshe Dayan; published many novels and also was a war correspondent during the Six-Day War; born in Nahalal

Abba (Aubrey) Solomon Eban (b. 1915-   ), diplomat and statesman, served as ambassador to the United States from 1950 to 1959 and later as foreign minister; born in Cape Town, South Africa

Levi Eshkol (1895-1969), helped found the state of Israel and served as its prime minister from 1963 until his death; born Levi Shkolnik in Ukraine, Russia; in 1914 moved to Palestine and worked as a farmer

Hayim (Chaim) Hazaz (b. 1898), Hebrew novelist; born in Kiev District, Russia

Theodor Herzl (1860-1904), father of political Zionism and the founder of the World Zionist Organization; born in Pest, Hungary

Marcel Janco (b. 1895), painter, established himself as a leader of progressive art in Jerusalem in 1940; his paintings are representative yet highly stylized; born in Bucharest

Ephraim Katzir (b. 1916), fourth president of the state of Israel; settled in Israel in 1922; born in Kiev, Ukraine, Russia

Golda Meir (1898-1978), prime minister of Israel from 1969 to 1974; born Goldie Mabovitch in Kiev of the Ukraine, now a republic of the Soviet Union; family moved to Milwaukee, Wisconsin in 1906; in 1921, went to Palestine and joined a collective farm village

Shimon Peres (b. 1923), became prime minister in September 1984; born in Vishnevo near Minsk, Poland (now Soviet Union); moved in 1934 with family to Palestine

Yitzhak Rabin (b. 1922), prime minister of Israel from 1974 to 1977 after winning fame as a military leader; born in Jerusalem, the nation's first prime minister to be born in Israel

Yitzhak Shamir (b. 1915), prime minister from October 1983 to September of 1984; became foreign minister in 1980; born in Ruzinoy, a village in eastern Poland; his last name was Jazernicki, later changed to Shamir, the Hebrew word for both "thistle" and "flint"

Zalman Shazar (b. 1889), Israel's third president; born in Mir, Russia

Anna Ticho (b. 1894), graphic artist, widely known for her delicate drawings in charcoal and pen and ink; born in Brno, Moravia, Austria

Chaim Weizmann (1874-1952), the first president of Israel, from 1949 until his death; born in Motol, Russia, and educated in Switzerland and Germany

PRESIDENTS

Chaim Weizmann	1949-1952
Itzhak Ben-Zvi	1952-1963
Zalman Shazar	1963-1973
Ephraim Katzir	1973-1978
Yitzhak Navon	1978-1983
Chaim Herzog	1983-

PRIME MINISTERS

David Ben-Gurion	1949-1953
Moshe Sharett	1953-1955
David Ben-Gurion	1955-1963
Levi Eshkol	1963-1969
Golda Meir	1969-1974
Yitzhak Rabin	1974-1977
Menachem Begin	1977-1983
Yitzhak Shamir	1983-1984
Shimon Peres	1984-1986
Yitzhak Shamir	1986-

INDEX

Page numbers that appear in boldface type indicate illustrations.

About the Author

Helen Hinckley Jones was born in Utah, granddaughter of four pioneers. The history of the American West was her major study in earning her B.S. and M.S. degrees, and five of her books have been in this field, including *Over the Mormon Trail (Childrens Press)*. Although Mrs. Jones has written five books about Old Testament heroes, this is her first book about present-day Israel.

Mrs. Jones has been honored by Pasadena City College, Brigham Young University, the Southern California Council on Literature for Children and Young People, and is listed in *Who's Who in the West* and *Who's Who of American Women*. She lives in Altadena, California with her husband, Ivan Charles Jones; her two daughters are married and she has nine grandchildren.